Living on
Less
and
Living it
More

OTHER BOOKS BY MAXINE HANCOCK:

Can I Really Have it All? (NavPress, 1991; reprint, Regent College Publishing, 1999.)

Child Sexual Abuse: A Hope for Healing. Co-author, Karen Burton Mains. (Harold Shaw Publishers, 1987; rev. ed., 1997).

Creative, Confident Children. (Revell, 1978; 1st rev. ed., Harold Shaw Publishers, 1991; 2nd rev. ed., Regent College Publishing, 2001).

Love Knows no Difference: Learning to Give and Receive. (Harvest House, 1983; reprint, Regent College Publishing, 1999).

Re-Evaluating Your Commitments. (First published as *The Forever Principle.* Revell, 1980; rev. ed. Bethany House, 1990; reprint, Regent College Publishing, 2001).

ACADEMIC:

The Key in the Window: Marginal Notes in Bunyan's Narratives. (Regent College Publishing, 2000).

Readings in Biblical Hebrew: An Intermediate Textbook. Co-authors, Ehud Ben-Zvi and Richard Beinert (Yale University Press, 1993).

Maxine Hancock

Living on Less and Liking it More

how to reduce your spending and increase your living

Regent College Publishing • Vancouver

Originally published 1976 by Moody Press, revised in 1994 by Victor
Books, and revised further in 2002.

Views expressed in works published by Regent College Publishing should
be regarded as the personal opinions of the individual authors rather than
as reflecting the official opinions or policies of Regent College.

National Library of Canada Cataloguing in Publication Data

Hancock, Maxine.
  Living on less and liking it more : how to reduce your spending and
increase your living / Maxine Hancock.

  Includes bibliographical references and index.
  ISBN 1-55361-062-8 (Canada)
  ISBN 1-57383-138-7 (United States)

  1. Christian life. 2. Materialism—Religious aspects—Christianity.
3. Values. 4. Cost and standard of living. I. Title.

BV4501.2.H32 2002   241'.68   C2002-911235-4

To
my parents,
MAX and RUTH RUNIONS,
who have known and shown
that
"godliness with contentment is
great gain"

CONTENTS

First, This Word

"When times are good, be happy; but when times are bad, consider" (Ecc. 7:14).

I did not set out to write a book in praise of poverty, for I find little about poverty to celebrate. I like the honesty of Samuel Johnson who is reported to have said, "While I was running about this town a very poor fellow, I was a great arguer for the advantages of poverty; but I was, at the same time, very sorry to be poor."

All the nostalgic reviving in books and television of the "good old days" when money was scarce but love was plentiful, all the romanticizing of the "pastoral dream" in which folks more or less effortlessly live off the land, leave me very unmoved. For nothing can blot out the fact that poverty is a sharply painful experience. I will have to leave to others the task of writing happy memoirs about the joys of voluntary poverty. We have had a taste of hardship — not that we exactly volunteered for it — and I consider poverty a state to be avoided. I can think of no more appropriate prayer for each other than that recorded by the loving Apostle John, "Dear friend, I pray that you may enjoy good health and that all may go well with you, even as your soul is getting along well" (3 John 2).

Nevertheless, my husband Cam and I did find "the day of adversity" to be a good time to consider and reconsider almost everything. And we have lived the many years since that time in the light of what we learned. Through a jolting business reversal, we came to an understanding of the problems of poverty and the joys of modest living. And we found that modest — and even meager — living could be a way of learning to re-examine our values and of learning to grow in love.

As young teachers, fresh out of university at a time when teachers were in great demand, we had enjoyed the comfort of regular and adequate wages. And then we decided to go farming. I still gulp hard when I type that and remember how, beginning with nothing, we set out to borrow the large amount of money necessary to begin a farming operation. Those first few years were rough. But we did manage to make our mortgage payments and meet basic needs — not only for ourselves, but for a family to which we were just then adding a new baby every couple of years.

And then, just as we were beginning to feel that we were getting on our feet financially, we saw an opportunity that was too good to miss. Forming a limited company with another couple, we operated a joint grain-growing and cattle-feeding operation. For three years our grain crops were fed through cattle. On paper, the plan looked foolproof, of course. But just as the loans we had taken to launch this larger enterprise began to mature and demand repayment, the cattle market slid into a deep depression. We had to sell our fattened beef animals at prices far below production costs. And when we awakened one August morning to find that we had also lost our entire crop to an unseasonably early frost, we ground to the sudden halt of insolvency. It was a terrible, frantic, lost, hope-less feeling—one that has become all too familiar in more recent years to many people in North America, as apparently sure jobs have vanished in corporate downsizing, and seeming-ly invincible enterprises have faltered.

Looking back now, we wonder if we would have kept what sanity we salvaged, had we not been able to laugh. We had a kind of black humor that helped us through—lines like, "Well, one thing's for sure, when the big depression hits, we're going to have had years of practice," or Cam's, "I just wish I'd listened to my folks and gone to university—then I could have been somewhere warm, wearing a tie." There was, of course, financial uncertainty built into both of our vocations, my writ-ing and Cam's farming.

Through all those hard days, we learned ... so much.

The reflections of this book were originally written "the morning after" the day of adversity. I wanted to share what we had learned—new values and attitudes toward life. But I am coming back to this book for yet another edition in quite different circumstances. When our children were in post-secondary training, we cinched in our belts again so I could return to graduate studies. For several years after I completed doctoral studies, we continued to spend our summers on the farm and our winters in a city where I could teach and write. During those years, Cam was involved in farm organizations and agri-cultural practices promoting soil conservation and ecologically responsible agriculture. Finally, Cam leased out our farmland, and I turned my attention to full-time teaching at Regent College in Vancouver, Canada, where I now teach Inter-disciplinary Studies and Spiritual Theology. Should I perhaps be writing a sequel, rather than a new edition? Maybe something really saleable, like *Living on More and Liking it Better?*

I remember a day when I walked down a country road into a biting winter wind and argued with myself about whether I should even finish the manuscript for the first edition. By the time I had finished writing it, we had extricated ourselves from the most acute stage of the financial collapse we had experienced; we had found off-farm jobs, income was beginning to trickle in from my writing, and I thought: why not just chuck it, and live out to the edges of whatever prosperity the Lord might bless us with? Because writing the book and publishing it was a kind of commitment, a binding of ourselves to live by those values we had bruised ourselves in learning, to carry forward into the rest of our life our sense of God's call to modest living, regardless of our means.

Now, nearly two decades after the first publication of this book, many of our younger friends are asking tough questions about what a Christian lifestyle should look like. Questions like:

- Shouldn't Christian values de-materialize our lives?
- How do we learn to say, 'Enough's enough'? And at what point should we be saying it?
- Isn't there more to life than an endless scramble for money and things? Isn't there some way we can learn again how to really live?
- How will we face Christ our Lord and Judge if we have lived selfishly in a hungry, needy world?

This book is for these young people — now young people who are trying to figure out how to measure their lives qualitatively rather than only quantitatively; young people who are evaluating their lives in the light of a renewed sense of responsibility to others.

The first edition of the book came out along with several other books that have raised our consciousness concerning global and personal responsibility: Doris Janzen Longacre's *More-With-Less Cookbook* (Herald Press, 1976) and Ronald Sider's *Rich Christians in an Age of Hunger* (InterVarsity Press, 1977) also brought practical and theological perspectives to the discussion of evaluating our accepted North American affluence. Some of my own thinking was touched off not only by our own circumstances but by Sherwood Wirt's *The Social Conscience of the Evangelical* (Harper and Row, 1968) and W. Stanley Mooneyham's *What Do You Say to a Hungry World?*

(Word, 1975). All of us began to take a second look at our kitchen counters and our grocery carts. Later books would continue the discussion of which this book is a part. Born in my own need to evaluate attitudes and habits in the face of economic hardship, it presses on to ask questions I am still working on answering: How do we respond to the poor who are always with us? How do we react when we ourselves are the poor? And when we're not? We are realizing that our choices as consumers do affect others' lives; that we are, as I believer, in this global village, our "brothers' and sisters' keepers" with a responsibility for the well-being of others as well as of our own selves and our families. We are all uneasily aware that deep changes in patterns of production and distribution have become essential. And so the discussion of this book continues to be timely.

I am writing out of our lives for those who are hurting financially; for those who are hurting in conscience, uneasily questioning their values and trying to find guidelines for a Christian lifestyle; and for Cam and me and for our children — all now twenty-somethings, launching themselves in diverse careers at a difficult time. What this book is about is *modest living*, about learning to live at a somewhat lower standard than what we have come to accept as the norm, about finding a balance point between poverty and riches where we can live in love to our Lord, to our families, to our world.

I write as a Christian, committed to living out my life under the Lordship of Jesus Christ, and according to the principles of the Bible, through which He continues to speak to me. What I have to say, however, may well be of interest to others who, while not sharing my religious convictions, find themselves in modest or even extreme circumstances. Whether they have come to be in such circumstances by the front door of idealistic choice or the back door of necessity, there are many who want to engage in the process of understanding a set of values that puts things in their place.

I invite you to join us on our journey toward life lived joyfully and, at least on our best days, not entirely selfishly.

ACKNOWLEDGMENTS

In preparing this book for this new edition, I continue to accrue debts of appreciation to people who have been generous with their time and wisdom. I consulted with Deanna Swinamer, a dietician and family physician who helped me with the revisions to chapter 7; University of Alberta Professor Bruce Wilkinson, international economist, and Greg Brandenbarg, international justice educator, who gave me their perspectives on the larger ecnomic issues facing us today; Lyle Larson, University of Alberta professor and family sociologist, who helped me with materials and resources and an ongoing conversation about the contemporary family.

In preparing earlier editions of this book, I was helped by editors Les Stobbe of Moody Press and James R. Adair of Victor Books. For this new edition, Rob Clements of Regent College Publishing has been unfailingly helpful: my thanks go to these, and to all who have believed in this book and its message enough to encourage me to present it again to a new readership.

And always, to Cam, who walks with me; to a circle of friends who encourage me; and to my students at Regent College who continuously challenge me, my continuing grateful thanks.

—Maxine Hancock
Regent College, 2002

Chapter One

The Call to Modest Living

It was Abe's illness that called Abe and Carole out of their comfort zone to work together in new ways and learn to trust God for things which they formerly had pretty much taken for granted.

The day I went to see them, they were enjoying the warmth and comfort of a new living-room rug, a Christmas gift from a member of their family. But the clean, neat room was sparsely furnished, and hard times were in evidence. Abe was still getting used to being blind, a result of hemorrhaging caused by diabetes. "It's not black," he explained. "It's just gray." But he couldn't see anything, not even the pretty faces of his little girls rapidly turning into young ladies, nor the face of his wonderful wife, Carole.

I sat there with them, trying to "sit where they sat," trying to imagine how we would react to such a problem. "Didn't you protest? Rebel? Cry out, 'Why me, God?' " I asked.

Abe shook his head. "God is God," he said simply. "And," he added, "I had a good model to follow when tough times came. We grew up in the dried-out prairies. I can remember years when there was no crop at all. But my folks used to plant potatoes in the slough beds, the only place where there might possibly be enough moisture to grow anything. And I can remember going out with my father to dig potatoes in the fall, and watching him stand there in that slough bottom and stop to thank God for the potatoes, for food for his family during the winter ahead. So I guess I learned early to accept and to trust."

And Carole explained, "I think it was harder for me to accept Abe's blindness than it was for Abe himself. He was really amazing. He just accepted that if this was his lot, he would have to learn to live with it."

They told me, together, of how they had learned lessons in the recent months of financial hardship that they had missed in the earlier years of their married lives.

"Like what?" I asked.

"Like the faithfulness of God. Everything we had ever believed was put to the test, and God is just as good as His Word declares Him to be. Time after time, we would have used our last dollar, and not have any idea where to turn, when the Lord would supply. Once it was by a letter in the mail. Another time — a Sunday morning — a friend pressed a gift of money into our hands when he shook hands with us at the end of the service."

"We learned, too," Abe told me, "how little material things really matter. Before I was blind, things mattered to me. A lot. Like, what kind of car I had, or my clothes." I had looked at the picture on the piano of a big, handsome Abe with Carole, his young bride, beside him. That other Abe, that Abe "before the darkness," had been a hard-working, self-reliant, things-oriented man, he told me. "But now," Abe said, "the only real things are the things of the spirit. I have learned to really *see* in another realm." He was thoughtful for a moment. "And it has made me appreciate my wife more than ever before."

To Abe and Carole — despite all of the financial problems, all the personal readjustments as Carole shouldered wage earning and Abe took up household tasks — the experience was summed up: "To us, this is not a tragedy but an opportunity." They have found in adversity an opportunity to really get to know God, an opportunity to reevaluate things, a new kind of opportunity for service.

Many people, like Abe and Carole, have had to face the economic results of severe illness or disability — a car accident, a kidney failure, a stroke, a heart attack. With the lost earning power come the often overwhelming medical expenses. Such circumstances may force the family to drastically revise its standard of living — sometimes permanently.

Others have had seemingly secure jobs wrenched from them by conditions beyond their control. During the past few years many people who had previously felt secure in their ability to earn a living have been forced into the emotional turmoil and economic difficulties accompanying job loss. Not the statistics in *Time* but the happy relief in my friend's voice as she told me, "We're happy — at least Tom still has work and can put the bread on the table —" tells the real tale of the threat of unemployment.

When the breadwinner (or breadwinners) of a family are out of work for even a few weeks or months, the call to modest living cannot be avoided. Many, having lost professional or skilled work, have to accept lower-paying jobs. And the standard of living must, often painfully, be adjusted to the new economic facts of the family's existence.

For others, retirement from the work force brings about an enforced revision — one that is often acutely painful — of their lifestyle. Many people now entering retirement experienced struggle during the early part of their earning years. Remembering the hard and lean years, they feel sharp anxiety at having once again, in old age and failing health, to suffer the effects of economic deprivation.

Others are hearing a less strident but just as unavoidable call to more modest living. For various reasons, many young people are considering seriously a call to a simple lifestyle. It is a way of freeing themselves from a materialistically motivated "rat race" in which some feel trapped; a way of living for values other than things; a way of conserving the limited resources of our small earth; or a way of making more money from their incomes available for sharing with those in need.

Annabelle and Ron, for instance, have been married for

about six years, enjoying the "Double-Income, No Kids" stage of life. Now Annabelle has left her university teaching career and is staying at home with their first child, excitedly learning about "child development" (along with "mother development") at close range. Ron is asking himself some hard questions about whether it is worth his while to cling to the high rung of the corporate ladder that he has reached. He has excellent wages as well as opportunities for travel and continuing education with the company for which he works. But his job absorbs his time and energy almost completely. And the company requires that he move periodically from one big city to another, in order to take increasingly responsible jobs.

"There's got to be more to life than this," he says thoughtfully. "I want to supply my family with more than just things. I want to share in their growing up, deeply and intimately." Right now it is just a dream, but Annabelle and Ron are thinking seriously about finding a way to work only part-time each and live modestly on a lower shared wage so that together they can enjoy more of the tasks of being parents.

Other young people have set the example. Twenty-five years ago, Will left a government job. He and his wife, Marion, each worked limited part-time hours — she at teaching nursing; he, as an economic consultant — to create a modest, pooled "living allowance." The rest of their energy went into creating a simple lifestyle on a small farm. Both having grown up in the country, they knew what they were doing and what sacrifices were required. "We can live together as a family this way," they said. "The children can know the joy of finding new kittens in the loft, and we can share that joy with them." The children have grown — and treasure the values Will and Marion passed on to them.

A Call to Modest Living

Thus, a new appreciation of the real needs of families is creating a call to more modest living for some. Another growing realization that is forcing itself upon our thinking is that the luxurious lifestyle which has been so generally adopted is, in large measure, responsible for the ecological problems we now face. Francis Schaeffer sees "hurry and greed" as the dual cause of most ecological damage:

> *Almost always,* the scar and the ugliness are the results of hurry. And whether it is hurry or greed, these things eat away at nature. But as Christians we have to learn to say "Stop!" Because . . . greed is destructive against nature at this point and there is a time to take one's time.[1]

With this awareness, many young people are altering their lifestyles, attempting to reduce their own personal consumption of the earth's resources.

Then, too, some young people are taking steps to live on less than what they earn in order that they might have more to share. In a Midwestern city, a doctor and his wife sold their large home in an exclusive district and relocated to a modest house in a working-man's section of the same city. They choose to drive a plain and aging car. They grow a garden. Now, with an income much larger than their reduced family needs, they are able to give generously to missions, world relief, and their local church. To them, the call of Jesus Christ was to a more modest lifestyle. They heard and responded with obedience.

While not all believers are being called to take such drastic action to change their lifestyles, many are looking for ways to trim the budget, to be more conservative in their spending, and thus, either to reduce their personal needs in order to live comfortably on a lower income, leaving them more time and energy for other pursuits compatible with their Christian commitment, or to leave themselves a wider margin of income over needs, from which they can share more bountifully with others.

The fact is that the Christian church in North America, which had become bogged down in the things-based value system which until recently dominated Western culture, is — slowly —

awakening to other values. More and more, Christians are becoming uncomfortably aware that some of the very basic principles of Christianity were sold or traded cheaply at a garage sale of values in mid-century. We are struggling back toward an emphasis on such things as love, compassion, and sharing.

The failure of a number of innovative communal living experiments formed during the rush of idealism in the late 1960s and 1970s should not blind us to the importance of having a range of models for the economic setup of homes and families. Intentional communities of various kinds, where people pool their resources in order to free some or all of the members for commitments to prayer or action — or both — continue to exist and to play their part in reminding us that we need to "be on [our] guard against all kinds of greed; a [person's] life does not consist in the abundance of his [or her] possessions" (Luke 12:15). And while the family is still the most functional basic economic cooperative, there are all kinds of variations on the traditional roles within the nuclear family which are reminding us that families have only recently become as isolated and nuclear as they now are.

When I was in the stage of grieving my empty nest, a woman came up to me after a conference session in which I had spoken and took my hand. "Don't be too sad," she said. "Nowadays, children come back!" Her words proved to be prophetic: Several years later, when our eldest son's wife left him with two preschool daughters, he and his little girls came "home to the farm." Since Geoff is a pilot who flies water-bombers in the Canadian north on a summer contract, we spend the summers at the farm not just farming, but also looking after two darling granddaughters. And now, our quite unintentional community also includes a sister whose marriage, after thirty-four years, has ended. In fact, we live like some sort of ancient tribe, with grandparents and great-aunts and motherless children all sharing one roof, dividing up the work and childcare and creating a safe and loving space for healing.

The high costs of post-secondary education, the difficulties of young people now emerging into adulthood in finding steady or long-term employment, and the frequency of marriage breakdown are forcing families back into intergenerational models in which adult children often live at home much longer than they used to, or return, singled, with children. At the same time, the rising cost of elder-care and the insufficiency of community resources to supply services is returning the care of the old to families too. This, along with the widespread incidence of fatal and epidemic diseases such as AIDS, may mean that families will be involved in nursing care. Futurists suggest that family homes will need to have "dying rooms" as well as living rooms, and "bounce back" rooms for family members recovering from marriage failure or job loss.

None of these changes is particularly comfortable. But Christians, of all people, should have the resources to respond to—at the very least—the needs within their own families. The call to modest living is being heard by many, in many ways. How to respond to that call, how to readjust values and reeducate tastes, and how to learn new habits and acquire new attitudes: that is the subject of the chapters that follow.

Chapter Two

The Golden Mean

Television brings us the pictures, but somehow it takes a personal encounter before I can understand the concept of the kind of deep poverty that two-thirds of the world lives in. I capture it better when it is put in word-pictures than I do from the television clips: Marilyn, returning after a couple of years in Haiti, saying, "You simply can't imagine how people, average people, live there. The average person expects to get maybe three meals *a week.*"

"A week?" I echo, hoping she has made a mistake.

"A week," she reiterates. And I realize that, although I have known times when buying the weekly groceries was a challenge in faith and careful management, our family has always had three meals a day.

Or Cam's descriptions of the two- or three-room farm homes he stayed in during a visit to a farming community in rural Mexico: the sparse tidiness of the best of them, the clutter and grime of the worst, as though there was a fear of throwing anything away in case it might, someday, be needed; the general despair of life ever being more than a struggle for daily subsistence. And I realize that, although I have lived in small farm homes, most of the Mexicans with whom Cam visited would have found them more than adequate, even spacious.

Or Wanjiku Kironyo's descriptions of the women's groups she works with in the Mathare Valley, the huge slum city that is the shadow-city to Nairobi in Kenya: women for whom the main concern is to find some other way to support their children than by brewing potently addictive cheap beer or prostitution; women for whom the important issues are whether they can feed their children, let alone supply shoes and school fees to keep their children in school. And I realize that, although I know what it is to wonder how I am going to afford winter overshoes for growing feet, I have never really wondered *if* they would have footwear or fees for school.

And so, in discussing "modest living," we run into an immediate difficulty. Just what is it? "Modest" compared with what? Where do we draw the line? At what point do we say "satisfied"? And by whose standard of comparison are we entitled to call our lifestyle modest? Do we measure our lifestyle against that of the Haitians? Or the hungry of North Africa or Bangladesh? Yet, how can we ignore the economic realities of the Western world which have given us such a high standard of living? Do we have to live in either self-inflicted poverty or self-induced guilt?

Stanley Tam, a highly successful businessman who has lived modestly and devoted his business profits to Christian causes, makes this telling comment:

> I am not a sackcloth-and-ashes Christian. We have a modest but comfortable home. My wife and I dress well. We are careful with money, never lavish in our spending. . . . It is characteristic of Americans—too often including American Christians—to adjust their living standards to their amount of income, usually keeping the former just a bit higher than the latter. But really, in this land which offers so much, where the poorest family in almost any community has more than the wealthiest family in some overseas areas . . . the thinking Christian needs to consider carefully that point at which he will be willing to say, "It is good enough."[1]

How do we, individually and as families, avoid becoming sackcloth-and-ashes Christians and yet enter into the joys of modest living? The voice of Wisdom speaks to us from the Book of Proverbs: "Give me neither poverty nor riches; but give me only my daily bread." The dangers of either extreme are summarized in the same proverb: "Otherwise, I may have too much and disown You and say, 'Who is the Lord?' Or I may become poor and steal, and so dishonor the name of God" (Prov. 30:8-9).

In wealth, the danger is independence of God. In poverty, the danger is a discouragement so profound that we are tempted to "curse God and die" as Job's wife suggested doing (Job 2:9).

What we are looking for in this whole consideration of modest living is something like the ancient Greek philosophical idea of the golden mean, that perfect balance point at which there is neither too much nor too little of anything. The New Testament refines this concept, telling us that, as believers, a hallmark should be "moderation" (Phil. 4:5). As believers, we have not only the challenge, but the indwelling power of the Holy Spirit, to enable us to live at that golden mean so long sought by the philosophers, that golden mean at which we have neither too much nor too little, but at which we have brought needs and supply into a comfortable balance. In our affluent society, that golden mean or balance point will probably best be reached through generous sharing of the good things with which we have been blessed.

Before we begin feeling a bit smug about the level at which we establish our own personal golden mean, we need to remind ourselves of the golden standard by which all giving, all cutting back, all sharing, must ultimately be measured:

> For you know the grace of our Lord Jesus Christ, that though He was rich, yet for your sakes He became poor, so that you through His poverty might become rich (2 Cor. 8:9).

Establishing a Standard of Living

I suggest three basic principles which might serve as a guide as we try to establish at what point in our standard of living we can reasonably say, "It is enough."

1. *Responsibility:* The concept of stewardship of all of our personal resources is central to any meaningful Christian commitment. And, of course, the idea that all we have is a gift to be held in trust carries with it the concept of accountability for the responsible use of those gifts. Paul writes what would have been known as common knowledge in a society where stewards managed large estates: "Now it is required that those who have been given a trust must prove faithful" (1 Cor. 4:2). To be a Christian is to operate in every area of life as a bonded person: one to whom money — or talents, or abilities, or opportunities — can be safely given in trust.

The Scriptures are full of the idea that the way in which we deal with material goods is, fundamentally, a spiritual matter. As I prepared to write this book, I read through the entire New Testament, marking every passage dealing with money or our attitude toward things with a yellow highlighter. I take up that old Bible now, and am still amazed to see how many pages are marked. The writers of Scripture have a great deal to say about material things. According to Harold J. Sutton, "Money and possessions are allotted much space in the Bible. In the Old Testament, it is one verse in six; in the New Testament it is one verse in seven. Sixteen of the parables of our Lord have to do with the stewardship of possessions."[2]

The parable that Jesus told about a lord's entrustment of his servants with varying amounts of money, weighed out in "talents," as told in Matthew's Gospel in chapter 25:14-30, is Jesus' classic discourse on the requirements and responsibilities of stewardship. What we are given we are responsible to use — not solely or even primarily for our own satisfaction — but for maximum profit to the Giver. The implication for those of us living in the wealthy northern half of the world is that we will have to answer for our use of that wealth. There are questions we have to confront — now or at some later judgment time: To what degree have we squandered it? Dug a hole and hid it, failing to invest it in improving the lives of others? Or have we recognized the trust which is ours and used whatever resources have been placed at our disposal wisely, investing not only for material, but also for spiritual returns?

The story Jesus told about entrustment may also be read to remind us that it is the right of the Master to give varying amounts in trust to his servants. From the letters of Paul and James, it is evident that rich and poor people met together in the early churches. (You might like to look at, for example, 1 Corinthians 11:18-22 and James 2:1-4 — passages which discuss courtesy and social sensitivity in an economically mixed situation, and 2 Corinthians 8:1-15 and James 2:14-17 for some discussion of what the apostles taught as the appropriate Christian response to the needs of others within the community.) Individual responsibility for meeting one's own needs and the needs of one's family is stressed in balance with an open-hearted and open-handed response to the needy beyond the immediate circle of family or even of only the local church. It will be in this context of individual and group responsibility that we will one day give account for the management of the material resources entrusted to us, as Jesus' teaching on the judgment of the nations as "sheep" or "goats" clearly shows (Matt. 25:31-46).

Modest living means that there is no financial state in which the responsibility of giving is lifted from us. The reality of this is borne out in a story recorded in Mark's Gospel. Jesus stood watching as people brought their money gifts to the temple. After a number of wealthy people had made large, clinking donations, a poverty-stricken widow put in two "very small copper coins." And Jesus said, "I tell you the truth, this poor widow has put more into the treasury than all the others. They all gave out of their wealth; but she, out of her poverty, put in everything — all she had to live on" (Mark 12:43-44). Jesus enunciated a principle of reality in the kingdom of God: that our giving is not measured by the amount we give, but by the amount we have left over when we have given. Giving from our wealth and plenty is one kind of giving, but giving from our poverty, sharing our "daily bread," is the kind of giving especially commended by the One whom, as Christians, we call Lord. Realism demands that we learn the deep pain and great joy of establishing a standard of giving that affects our standard of living.

2. *Restraint:* Living modestly by choice means making decisions about spending and giving that establish our standard of living somewhere below the level we could enjoy if our income were administered entirely for the needs and desires of ourselves and of our families.

People who choose to live modestly refuse to be coerced by television and other advertising into feeling that everything five years or older is obsolete and in need of replacement. When shopping to replace our fifteen-year-old living room furniture (which, in the end, we decided to reupholster rather than replace), we were startled to be told that the average North American family refurnishes major areas of a home every four to five years. Actually, I expect that's more wishful thinking on the part of furniture-makers than an actual reality ... or maybe we're living even farther behind — or below — the average than I have realized.

A visit to countries in which living and business is carried on in buildings many hundred years old is a sobering corrective for our North American "new is better" mentality, where the swinging demolition ball is a symbol of progress. Friends of ours who have spent their lives in Europe have pointed out to us that our feeling that a car is "old" simply on the basis of its year or mileage is also idiosyncratically North American, out of line with the thinking in much of the rest of the world. "There's nothing wrong with the upholstery, is there?" our friend asked, walking around our ancient half-ton truck. "And the exterior is not rusted out, is it? So what if it has 150,000 miles on it? There's nothing that can't be fixed to make it run another 100,000 miles. A car like this wouldn't be considered old in Europe." Let alone in Mexico, we have come to realize, or in the Caribbean or South America.

Living with restraint means planning rather than impulse

buying; assessing "wish lists" to discriminate between needs and wants; and evaluating one's own needs and desires in the light of the needs of others. That's no easy matter, since probably every purchase we make could be scrutinized by someone and found to be excessive. It means living in some kind of uneasy tension between the *via positiva* — the way of grateful celebration of the good things of life, and the *via negativa* — the way of self-abnegation and self-emptying on behalf of others. In learning to live under the principle of restraint in our spending habits, we have to resist not only the voices that tell us, "Want it? Buy it," but also the voices that tell us that everything delightful borders on the sinful, that we should not enjoy the good things of life. It is precisely in the matter of sharing our material goods that the Apostle John writes, "If our hearts do not condemn us, we have confidence before God" (1 John 3:21). Living with restraint means that, having worked out a decision to buy in the light of the principles of responsibility and restraint, we need not live in continual guilt about the things we do decide to buy, but in joyful, grateful enjoyment.

And living with restraint may mean that we are free to make at least some of our decisions on some basis other than economic maximization. A job that may have high earning potential may be turned down for one in which one earns less but is doing work that is more satisfying, more fully fulfilling one's deep sense of vocation or call. Some of these considerations were involved when, after we had reestablished our personal finances and repaid our debts, Cam and I spent a lot of time pondering how we should order the second half of our adult lives. The road of economic maximization was clear: We could both get teaching jobs, hold them for another twenty years, and rent out the farmland as an additional source of income. But Cam's love for the land and his deep vocation or call to nurture life — not to mention his penchant for risk-taking — called him into a new commitment to his farming as a full-time occupation. My hunger for learning and my need to write, as well as to do some part-time teaching, called me to go back to the university for graduate work. And so we again combined precarious income sources, needing to continually exercise tight-reined fiscal management and restraint. But we wake up every morning with the exhilaration of knowing that we are both able to do what we love to do, what we are called to do. And, we remind ourselves, our seven-year-old car is still not old by world standards.

The restraint in spending that we learned in very hard times has become a matter of choice, with the result that we have had more freedom in making career choices than many of our age-mates. Recently, when considering and turning down a "steady job," I found myself saying, "Since I'm willing to be poor, I am free to go on exploring." Being free to choose to continue contract and freelance work with all of its uncertainty and challenge was an outcome of having learned to live within the constraints of uncertain income. And even though we sometimes chafe at the restrictions of living within a limited and unpredictable income, Cam and I realize that we are quite wonderfully free.

3. *Realism:* Living modestly requires a strong sense of realism, something which is often dulled by easy credit and high-pressure advertising. It means living within our budgets, whether they are limited by necessity or by choice. With accessible credit and continual inducements to buy, it is possible for a family to live beyond its means, keeping up an appearance of prosperity in excess of real earnings, at least for a period of time.

Modest living also means living with a sense of realism and responsibility toward those to whom we owe money. We are under the same instructions as were given to the Christians in ancient Thessalonica — to live "so that your daily life may win the respect of outsiders," — meaning to conduct our business in a way which is aboveboard in the eyes of the larger community (1 Thes. 4:12). The name of our Lord has been made light of and the effectiveness of the church has been seriously impaired by the cavalier attitude of many who call themselves Christians in matters of business ethics. "My dad always warned me to look out for anyone carrying a Bible," a neighbor told me, and I felt sad as I acknowledged that many nonbelieving people have higher standards when it comes to conducting their business affairs than do some who call themselves by the name, "Christian." *Realism* in our business affairs means, at the very least, honoring incurred debts and operating ethically and honestly in all of our business affairs.

Realism also means recognizing the needs of those who depend upon us. "If anyone does not provide for his relatives, and especially his immediate family, he has denied the faith and is worse than an unbeliever" is Paul's strong statement on the matter (1 Tim. 5:8). We must realistically provide for the needs of our children and of aged members of our families. Such provision has an indisputable *a priori* claim on our finances. Some of Jesus' harshest words were said to those who excused themselves from obligations to their aging parents by claiming that their money was "Corban," or dedicated to a religious purpose (as described in Mark 7:11-12). As we more and more frequently encounter the neglect of old people by their families, we need to live out our faith in honoring the needs of our own kin. There is truth in the old folk saying that "Charity begins at home." Realistically, if charity—not in the sense of pity or duty, but in the practice of need-meeting love—does not start there, it does not start at all.

Basically, then, modest living is an orientation toward income and standard of living rather than any specific point on the line between poverty and wealth. No single inflexible standard can be set, for what is modest living for people with large earning power may still be out of reach for others with less. The concept of modest living does not suggest that there is anything wrong with enjoying the good things of life as they are entrusted to us. I have composed psalms of thanksgiving—admittedly, some of them quite mawkish, but nonetheless sincere—for my automatic household appliances, grateful for the hours they have freed up from household chores for other pursuits. I still rejoice as I lift clothes out of the perma-press cycle of a clothes drier, realizing that I have written books in the hours that previous generations of women spent at the scrub board and the ironing board.

While we lived in a very cramped rented house, Cam and I looked forward to God's provision of a home big enough for our family of four fast-growing children. He did supply that home. We planned it with loving, prayerful care, making careful modifications to make a modest standard plan meet the particular needs of our family. And when the house was built, we moved into it (with, I remember so well, our two preschoolers with chicken pox and no hot water turned on yet) with thanksgiving and joy that have never stopped. It was perhaps just because we waited so long to have a home of our own, or perhaps because we built modestly enough to be able to feel not a single pang of guilt and to be able to pay off the mortgage in ten years, or perhaps because the plan we chose and modified has suited our family needs so well that we have to feel the Lord heard our request for divine guidance while we labored over the plans. Or perhaps just because for us it is, finally, home. Whatever the mix, our little white-stuccoed bungalow with chocolate brown trim has been a source of great joy and much praise.

In the process of buying our home, as in our other expenditures over the years, we have learned that nagging feelings of guilt about physical comforts disappear if the good things we have are not had at the expense of others; and if the good things we enjoy are truly within our means and are not just a result of setting ourselves adrift on a sea of credit.

Modest living is not so much a renunciation of specific things in themselves as it is a refusal to make things a goal in life or a source of ultimate satisfaction. It is the exercise of *responsibility, restraint,* and *realism:* whether our means are large or small.

Neither Poverty nor Riches

People who have lived cross-culturally have found that the general level of unhappiness seems to be nearly as great in affluent North America as in poverty-stricken countries of the world. Perhaps it is just a reality that too much money makes people as miserable as too little, that there is perhaps a happy medium at which basic needs can be met without undue anxiety, but at which that endless list of things-to-be-had is simply out of reach. Such a happy medium might be something close to the "golden mean," that balance point most conducive to human happiness.

It is a struggle to find such a balance point in our economic lives. Perhaps we will only begin our search for it when we realize that the only real satisfactions in life can never come from things—no matter how many or how lovely. Real satisfaction comes from relationships, of which the central and most deeply satisfying one is to be in communion with our Creator.

We are invited into such a relationship—the one for which we most deeply yearn and yet for which we so often attempt to substitute the procurement of things—through a life-changing, life-shaping commitment to Jesus.

Where might we start in re-evaluating our attitudes toward things? The Bible word—the word that Jesus proclaimed—is "Repent, for the kingdom of heaven is near" (Matt. 4:17). *Repent* does not mean to weep, or to "come forward" in a meeting—although it may be manifested in such actions or emotions. *Repent* means, simply, to make an about-face, a 180-degree change of direction. It means to turn away from what we have been seeking and to look in an entirely different direction for our sense of meaning and satisfaction in life. We might pray something like this:

Creator God, You made this good world and everything in it. I admit to You that I have too often been caught up in the things You have made and too little concerned with knowing, loving, and serving You. Forgive me, I pray. I want to know You more fully and love You more wholly—and to be set free from my preoccupation with things—no matter how legitimate they may seem to be in themselves. Through Jesus Christ Your Son and my Lord, I pray.

Chapter Three

Contentment: Learned, Not Earned

I was pulling up to a stop sign recently when I heard the commentator on the radio discussing a poll in which people had been asked how much money they felt they needed to earn in order to be comfortable. I did a quick mental calculation and had a figure in mind when the voice on the radio went on to say, "Most people felt they needed exactly double what they are now earning in order to be content."

I had to laugh at myself: the figure I had calculated in my mind was just that—double what last year's income tax figure had been. I fit right into the stereotype the survey had discovered, sharing the prevalent discontent—or, at the very least, disequilibrium—with the status quo. As my sister-in-law Marg pointed out to me many years ago, even the Apostle Paul had to say, "I have *learned* to be content" (Phil. 4:11, emphasis added). "Maybe it didn't come any easier to Paul to be content than it does to me," Marg said, "but it is a lesson that can be learned."

Contentment Can Be Learned
Contentment does not come easily to our hearts. I suppose from the very moment that the human heart lost communion with the Creator, we have all tried to stuff that empty yearning with things: things desired, things worked for, things even

worshiped. So contentment does not just come naturally to most of us. But it can be learned.

Contentment is probably the closest state we can reach to something like happiness. It is a quiet plateau that can be reached internally even when there seems little external reason for it. I remember visiting with Brian and Laura, a farm family, on a neighboring farm before Cam and I were married. The kitchen was sparse in a way I didn't know still existed — like something out of *Little House on the Prairie,* but this was 1960, not 1890. The kitchen was dominated by the wood stove, on which the cooking was still done; most of the chairs pulled out to the plain wood table had no backs. But the farm wife cheerfully served hot, black coffee and fresh buns, and the husband talked about life with a serenity I have only rarely encountered. Clearly, Brian and Laura had learned contentment.

But I have found it to be a difficult lesson to learn, and one which I have to relearn from time to time. In our affluent society, we live with the continual delusion that with "just one thing more" (or double our current income), we would be perfectly content. And so we are kept perpetually unhappy, perpetually off-balance, perpetually more concerned about things than we are about the more important issues of life — like our relationships with each other and with God.

"If only we had —" is an ongoing game of fill-in-the-blank. We discover through life that as we move into that bigger house, earn that larger income, wear those more stylish clothes, we are still the same discontent people — still being urged, as were our first parents in the Garden, to desire, and reach, and take.

When I first wrote this book, my own children were small, and I told this story:

> As I am writing these lines, my four-year-old is speaking to me from the kitchen where he is folding up newspapers he had spread out on the floor for spatter painting. "What is it, Mitchell?" I call.

He walks into the room where I am typing, holding a folded newspaper and studying an ad wistfully. "I wish we had a snowmobile," he says. And I sigh deep down inside, realizing how hard it is for those of our rich generation to enter the kingdom of spiritual values and to really understand how little *things* do mean.

My memory flashes back to the days, soon after we had completed our studies at the university, when Cam thought aloud, "I wish I had a snowmobile." They were fairly new on the popular market then, and in our long, snowy winters it's not hard to rationalize a "need" for such a recreational vehicle. Cam was earning a good wage; he was entitled to what our nephew Terry once called "a man's toy." But it wasn't long before the possibilities of the "toy" were exhausted. And every snowdrift started to look like every other snowdrift, and every race to feel like every other race. The snowmobile — finally sold to someone else — stands in our minds as a lifelong reminder of how unsatisfying individual things are.

Now it is our granddaughters who look yearningly at the catalogs and say, "I wish I had . . . ," and the sigh I sigh is the same. How hard, how very hard it is for us or for our little ones to find contentment in an affluent, thing-clogged world.

Nor is the problem anything new. David Grayson, the pseudonymous author of *Adventures in Contentment,* a quaint and interesting book published in 1906 and given to me by an elderly "gentleman farmer" of our district, tells how, from the age of seventeen, Grayson was driven "always forward, toward that vague Success which we Americans love to glorify." Then a serious illness arrested him, and he moved into a much slower existence. He says,

> I remember walking in the sunshine, weak yet, but curiously satisfied. I that was dead lived again. . . . And I possessed . . . a knowledge of a former exis-

tence, which I knew, even then, I could never return to.[1]

His basic discoveries on which he built this contentment were:

That we are not, after all, the slaves of things . . .
that we are not the used, but the users; that life is
more than profit or loss.[2]

Contentment, as expressed by this young man, and by others whom I know who have had close scrapes with death, is really a matter of living "on the other side of death." For the early Christians, the experience of baptism was a physical enactment of their entering into Christ's death, burial, and resurrection (see Rom. 6:3-4). As the new believers came up from the baptismal waters, hair and face streaming, they were dramatizing their entry into a new life, a life lived on the other side of death. Surely this is the image—as well as the reality—which lies behind Paul's words to the Colossian believers:

Since, then, you have been raised with Christ, set your
hearts on things above, where Christ is seated at the
right hand of God. Set your minds on things above, not
on earthly things. For you died, and your life is now
hidden with Christ in God (Col. 3:1-3).

Each summer, when our small village church gathers as a family for a weekend of fellowship at a sapphire-blue northern lake, its shape carved by glacial ice and its waters cold all summer, we celebrate the coming-to-faith of new believers with that ancient rite of baptism. The dramatic reenactment of God's act of grace in uniting each of us with our Lord in His death, and through Him bringing us into new life, reestablishes perspective and sharpens the focus for all of us. As the soaked and chilled confessors stumble back to the shore, we wade out to meet them, to wrap them in towels and in our arms. Risen to new life, made part of a new family, welcomed to the sandy shore—as one day we will be welcomed by those who have gone before us, when we go through that final baptism of death and find ourselves risen, washed and new in that final realization of "home" and "family" that is heaven. We who welcome the new believers into the community of faith are reminded again of our own baptismal confessions, of the newness of life into which we have entered—and are, each time, challenged anew to consider that since we have died, and our life has been "hidden with Christ in God," we have an invitation—and an obligation—to live with our hearts and minds set on "things above" rather than on the things and toys of this life.

Some of us—like me—are slow learners. We seem to have to "die" a little every day. Perhaps there are ways of shortening the learning process, of leaping to the mature understanding of how trivial things of this world are and how meaningless are the little toys for which we strive and struggle. For David Grayson, mentioned earlier, the shortcut was a face-off with death itself. For some it may be a dark night of the soul in which we learn full surrender and cry out, "All that I have and am and want, I give to You, my Lord and Master." Perhaps for the rest of us it has to be a matter of taking the things one at a time, as they present themselves to our minds in a delusion of delight, and dying to them—literally dying to the desire for that particular thing. And then, as one thing after another is passed by and we die to the desire that was kindled within us, we will gradually reach a habit of laying things before God without the long struggle of soul.

Cam and I call this attitude "holding things on an open hand."

We remember how one of our children had, as a toddler, clutched a piece of candy we had told her not to take. Such defiant, tightly curled little round fingers! We think of how we had to pry those little fingers, one by one, away from that treasure. It would have been so much easier for her—and for us—if she had held it out to us on an open hand and let us take it.

Job showed the attitude of "holding things on an open hand"

when he cried out, "The Lord gave, and the Lord has taken away; may the name of the Lord be praised" (Job 1:21). The earlier in life we learn to stop grabbing, clutching, and holding tightly, and the sooner we learn to hold all of life's good things in an open hand, the more easily and gently God can deal with us as His children. That's another way of saying that the more we live "on the other side of death," as Paul describes it in Romans 6, the less we will be attached to temporal, material things.

I will always remember the Sunday when the usher on our aisle in church held the offering basket out to our family. He noticed that little Heather Ruth, barely two at the time, was clutching something tightly. Assuming that she had been given money to be put in the plate, he held the basket quietly in front of her. Blue-eyed, round-cheeked Heather looked gravely from the plate to the usher, then down to her tightly clenched fist. And then, just as gravely, she moved her hand over the offering plate and let go what she was holding. The usher was as startled as I was to see, lying in the offering basket, a tiny paper figure of a blue-swaddled baby Moses—a treasured item from the take-home things she had been given in Sunday School. We smiled—but with tears just back of our eyes—for Heather had opened her hand to give something very precious to her.

I have found in many instances that God has waited patiently for us to move some desire from a position of central importance to the fringes of our minds—in short, no matter how reasonable or precious, to let it go—before letting us have that very item. He seems to grant "things" only when we are living relative to them, "on the other side of death," dead to them as goals, as status symbols, as sources of satisfaction, and accepting them only as means of bringing pleasure and praise to the One who has created all things (see Rev. 4:11).

Maybe one of the deepest instincts in a woman is a nesting instinct: a desire to have a suitable place in which to raise her brood. As a European friend put it: "For myself, I care not at all about things. Pff! You can have anything I have; I do not care. But for my children, it is different. Children make one bourgeois." This instinct is right and proper. Yet, like all of our good basic instincts, it can be turned against us and against God if we do not guard our lives carefully. Our need for a nesting place can become an obsession. Our definition of "adequate" can be raised to levels to which we may really have no right — merely by turning the pages of *Better Homes and Gardens* or by driving through those mouth-watering "exclusive" areas of our cities.

When we moved out to the old farmhouse where Cam had been raised, I said to him, "Don't ever ask me to move again." I put my roots down, right alongside the towering pine that stood close to the front veranda. The house was old, at least in western Canadian terms. It had been built soon after the turn of the century, and a lean-to had been added somewhere along the way. The kitchen occupied the lean-to, with a floor so sloped that anything which spilled landed up against the south baseboards. Upstairs were two bedrooms, both built under the eaves with steeply sloping walls; a tiny niche which in the old days had been — in the most strictly limited sense of the word — a *bathroom*, just big enough for an old-fashioned tub, and a walk-in closet or "drying room" with a tiny windowed dormer. Into this upstairs we tucked ourselves with first three and then four children, turning the niche into crib space and later building a double-decker bunk into it and painting and papering the "drying room" to make a tiny bedroom off ours.

There were saving virtues about the old place with its torn screens and loose windowpanes. Such as a large living room which, despite a sagging ceiling that made us wonder just what day the upstairs would come downstairs, had a fieldstone fireplace; a lovely big bathroom-utility room on the main floor, created out of one of the downstairs bedrooms when the house had been "modernized" late in its career. And, best of all, a downstairs bedroom adjoining the living room that worked perfectly for a study-office for me. Outside, the old house was peeling, the veranda sagging. But inside, there was warmth and love and happiness. And while I racked my brains trying to think of ways to expand our living space around the needs of our growing children, I had no intention of moving. Ever.

And then Cam, who had been increasingly distressed with a continuous hay fever reaction, went to an allergist. Skin tests were done, and the allergist was ready with his diagnosis. "Do you by any chance live in an old house?" he asked. Cam nodded. Yes, we lived in an old house.

"Ah!" the allergist exclaimed. "There's your problem. You are allergic to the sort of molds which accumulate between the walls of old houses, especially walls where moisture can seep in. Your strongest reaction is to such molds. I strongly advise that you get into a new house."

(I was shocked, some years after the publication of the first edition of this book, to discover that an editor who had worked on the manuscript had envisioned these molds as something visible growing *on* our walls—like some kind of fungus or moss. Please understand: these were invisible molds, growing *between* the walls—not on the outside of them. Had they been visible, we would have tried to solve our problem with a scrub brush and a good strong disinfectant!)

The doctor's diagnosis and prescription shattered my contentment. If Cam was sick in the house we lived in, and if a new house was necessary to his good health, wasn't it obvious that the Lord had indicated that we should build a new house? Obvious—to me. Not so obvious, unfortunately, to Cam.

Because what was more obvious to Cam than it was to me was that the business was going badly. That we were selling cattle at a loss. That we had debts that were going to be hard to meet. And Cam could not face building a new house—even on doctor's orders—while telling people that he could not afford to pay his bills. And so we were stalemated. For perhaps the first time in our marriage, our ability to communicate and to come to an understanding seemed to break down completely.

And then, the Lord provided us with a house.

Not, like in some people's stories, a big, new house that somehow a kindly rich person had a sudden need to sell at some inexplicably low price, although, believe me, I imagined such provision as I prayed. Nothing like that. God provided an *old* house, squarer and better built than our previous one, even more picturesque, and for rent. I, who had framed my request to the Lord as my "Three S Prayer" — for space, settledness, and security — found myself moving from one old farmhouse to another old farmhouse about a third smaller; from one where I felt sure I could live out my life, to one in which we would have three months' notice if a member of the landlord's family needed it; from one which we owned, to one which we could only rent. Talk about insecurity! I felt like a hen that couldn't quite settle back on the nest for fear it might suddenly be jerked away from under her.

If the tears had flowed as I walked down the winter lane of our own home, trying to figure out how to cope with Cam's illness and adamantine attitude about building a new home, now I found tears starting without notice as I tried to get things tucked into this latest domicile. I somehow could not reconcile myself to this as God's way of answering my prayer.

To make things worse, the house we moved into had a "reputation." It had belonged to a well-to-do city businessman who lived in the country. And since it was set well back from the road, down a pine-lined drive and in a beautiful parklike yard, people thought I was wonderfully lucky to be moving into such a grand house. "That's a beautiful big old house," they would comment.

"Beautiful, yes," I would reply. But big, definitely not. My hardest adjustment was having no study to work in. My filing cabinets were out in the unheated veranda; my desk and typewriter were stuffed into our small bedroom alongside the bed. That was harder for me to cope with than the ten-by-thirteen-foot combination kitchen-dining room with *five* doors leading off it. Or the bats that did not always stay up in the attic.

Why? Why? Why? What could possibly make this move right? Trying to make the best of things, I buoyed myself up through each week. We had moved closer to the center of the farming operation, so Cam could be home for lunch and supper with us. That was good, especially since for the previous two years he had left early in the morning and not returned until 10 P.M. or later at night all through the cropping season, becoming a virtual stranger to the children. And his allergy symptoms were definitely less acute. I was grateful for those things. Yet, each Sunday, when the kids had excused themselves after dinner and were out playing in the yard and Cam and I still sat across the table that took up about half of the tiny — although very pretty and freshly painted — kitchen, the tears would come. And the questions. And the anger. Cam was unmovable. He could not see how we could afford to build a house at that time.

And then one Sunday afternoon, I walked away from the table in anger. There wasn't very far that I could go in the house to get away from Cam, but I went into the bedroom adjoining the kitchen and threw myself, sobbing, onto the bed. And then, as I quieted, things began to come into focus for me.

Such unhappiness, I knew, was not coming from the Lord. I was angry and rebellious and wretchedly unhappy. And then, the gift of imagination helped me see into a possible future. I imagined what it would be like if I did coerce Cam into complying with my wish for a new home. Suppose we went ahead and built? Suppose then, that as Cam now feared, the house became a fearful financial burden? Suddenly I could picture us growing apart in a house big enough for us to really get apart from each other, with our love killed by my demands. And just imagining any size or shape of house without the love and joy which, through all the "better or worse" situations since we had been married, had been our mainstay, was convincing to me.

I prayed, then, something like this: *I don't feel like accepting this situation, Lord. It seems upside-down to me. It seems to me that we need a home now — not someday when the kids are grown and gone. But I am willing to wait for You to communicate that need to Cam without my demanding or badgering.* I felt like I was dying, and on that particular issue, I was.

When at last my weeping was over and my heart felt calm,

yet still very sore from the struggle, I went back to the kitchen.

Cam was still sitting there, nursing a cup of now-cold tea with a hurt and bewildered, angry look on his face. I sat down across from him and reached for his hand—a big, square, capable hand I had loved at first sight so many years before. "Cam," I said, "I'm all finished. I've said everything I'm going to say about 'house.' You won't hear me say that word again until you say it first."

And then I found myself "living on the other side of death" on that particular matter. Joy began to flow back into my life.

The little house was no less crowded, but now I could enjoy its charm and beauty. No longer threatened by my demands, Cam was able to begin to share his problems and concerns with me, and communication between us gradually became the deep, intimate sharing we had known before. I learned, again, that love and contentment are all that are really necessary to turn an "inadequate" house into a happy home.

The next few months fully vindicated Cam's determination not to assume any further debt for a house. When the farming business failed—an outcome that I had not realized was as imminent as Cam had—we were set to weather a financial storm that could have capsized us had we also been trying to pay for a new home. Our personal credibility with our creditors was high because we were living stringently, and they were remarkably patient with us. The little rented house was inexpensive, which helped to keep our living costs to a minimum. And all through that winter, the long hard winter of psychological restoration after a business failure, we thanked God for our snug and inexpensive accommodation. Debt we faced. Problems we had. But, as we lived close together in the small house, we experienced the joy of simple things: of enough money to buy a week's groceries, of enough money to pay the month's rent, of peace and joy and love between ourselves. What might have been "the winter of our discontent"—apart from the transforming work of the Holy Spirit—we shall always remember as the winter of recovery and healing.

In our financial setback, the Lord weeded out from Cam's heart, one by one, things that may have become too dear to him. The big tractors and trucks and equipment had to be sold as we liquidated assets to try to cover liabilities. And, at the same time, just as relentlessly, the great Gardener weeded from my heart the need, the burning desire, for a big new house.

We are still in the process of learning "how to get along happily whether [we] have much or little." But on some matters, at least, we are living on the other side of death. I do not want to give the impression that the learning process has been fun, or the lessons learned easily. But the Spirit of God is a thorough and loving Teacher. And, since all the other joys of life are actually dependent upon contentment, it is contentment we need most to learn.

At any level of income we can be inwardly gnawed by discontent. Most of us are still tricked into thinking we would be comfortable at just double our current rate of earning. But probably you have encountered, as I have, those few people who—apparently regardless of level of income—enjoy quiet contentment. From these encounters, I have become convinced that contentment cannot be earned. But I also know—from painful experience that has opened out onto lasting joy—that, even by such a slow learner as I, contentment can be learned.

Chapter Four

Living on Love

You cannot live on love. But it is even harder to live without it. And when a family—by choice or necessity—cuts back its standard of living, it needs to work at raising its standard of loving. Economic hardship is an experience that serves to prove, and to improve, love more than any other experience can. Of course, it often works the other way too. Economic problems are cited as a major contributing factor to a great many marriage breakdowns.[1]

So, if you are facing financial restructuring—for whatever reasons—you need to make sure your marriage is weather-proofed for the storms. Clear and honest communication becomes extremely important at such times. When people feel called to exercise restraint in their spending in order to give more, or to improve their quality of life by having time for other priorities—or just to get out of debt and start over—they need to work out the details of their situation carefully and come to an agreement about how they are going to cut their spending. If a husband and wife do not fully share the goals for which they are reducing their standard of living, and come to agreement about the extent of that reduction, it is hard to avoid bitterness. When Bob, a prosperous dentist, decided to give up his practice to assume a church-related ministry, his wife found the "call" hard to accept.

"Is it a full-time job he's going to?" I asked.

"Yes," she told me. "At a half-time salary." She went along with the change, but with little joy in the new status quo.

No matter how altruistic we may be in our ideals, we have to go on making our way in some sector of the culture in which we live. Crushing financial worries are no blessing. Nor is continual tension or arguing about what constitutes a legitimate expenditure. And because money-making and money-disposing are so tightly tied up with self-esteem in our culture, money discussions may need to be prefaced with an assurance: "We're not talking about each other, and we're not talking about our marriage. We're talking about how we are going to organize our finances." Cam calls this "putting the issue out on the table" — separating the discussion from ourselves and, as much as possible, from potentially explosive emotional elements. Most of us have learned (by communications training or by hard experience) that it is wiser to send "I" messages: "I feel as though you disapprove of the way I am handling the grocery budget," rather than "you" messages: "You always act as though I spend too much for groceries." Careful listening to each other, with feedback loops like, "Do I hear you saying . . . " and, sometimes, the decision to postpone a discussion until both parties are more rested or under less immediate pressure can help to moderate the "climate" of painful but necessary discussions.

If the cutback is not one of choice, but one which is forced upon you, then clear and complete honesty in communications becomes even more imperative. As long as either partner tries to pretend that there are no problems, that life can go on as it has been, the family will live in a position which is at odds with reality and which is therefore untenable. Honesty with each other is a necessary prerequisite to honesty with the outside world.

Family Communication

When there are children in the family, some of the communication has to be with them. They should not be loaded with worrisome details, but they need to understand the general outline of the reality the family is facing.

As the condition of our business gradually became public knowledge—and there are few secrets that can be kept in a rural community—our children had to field questions from friends at school. One day, Geoffrey, then nine, came into the house.

"Dad," he asked, sounding extra casual, "is our company going broke?"

"Why?" Cam asked.

"Well, because Grant told me it was folding up."

"He's right, Geoff," Cam replied.

"What does that mean?"

Cam explained carefully but simply to Geoff the way in which cattle-market conditions and a killing August frost on our crops had worked together to bring the company to a position where it was unable to repay its obligations without selling all of its machinery and other assets.

It isn't easy to say to children, "We just can't afford it," but that year we had to tell our children just that; not only about such things as the Christmas goodies in the stores and catalogs, but about items far more basic, such as winter overshoes.

We simply didn't have the money to outfit all eight feet, and they all needed new boots. So we told the children about the situation, and as a family we prayed about it. Each child prayed for his or her own winter boots, some giving specifications as to the type they would prefer. The Lord answered first by delaying snow. In our Alberta winters, we usually have permanent snow by the first week of November. That winter, no snow fell and stayed until December 22. And by that time, we had received a small check that covered the cost of on-sale overshoes for all eight feet. Not, mind you, the bush boots Geoffrey had requested. Nor the side-zipped tall boots of Cammie's desire.

But, for all the children, warm and acceptably styled winter footwear. The children learned to enjoy the Lord's provision and give thanks along with us. It was an experience for all of us in learning neither to take the good, basic provisions we needed for granted, nor to demand the supply of every whim. And best of all, when we talk together about those days, the children remember them as snug and happy years – not as years of deprivation or hardship.

Dealing with Blame and Anger

Economic pressures do create a need and an opportunity for a family to really pull together. Or a situation in which a family falls apart. When the going gets rough, I expect that everyone has to fight against the desire to lay blame.[2] If only *someone* hadn't made that particular business decision; if only *someone* didn't need to spend so much on clothes. But that "root of bitterness," if ever allowed to develop, will be destructive: if not of the marriage itself, certainly of the love that sustains it. It's like the red-rooted pigweed that we fight in our gardens in the countryside where I live: a tiny plant at first, but one that puts down a long root and sucks the moisture and nutrition away from anything growing near it.

I know I struggled with blaming (sort of like a long game of "pin the tail on the donkey" – any donkey but me). I tried blaming Cam, the neighbor who was our business partner, the markets, the weather. I was too pious, of course, to even think of blaming God. So I was pretty startled one day as I did my daily Scripture reading (for some reason I was plowing my way through the Pentateuch that winter) to be sharply reminded that when Israel complained against Moses, they were actually grumbling against God. This struck me as I read through Exodus. The response of Moses and Aaron to the complaining Israelites was straightforward: "The Lord . . . has heard your grumbling against Him. Who are we, that you should grumble against us?" (Ex. 16:6-7) God's attitude toward His complaining children in the desert is echoed and applied by Paul in the first letter to the Corinthian Christians: "We should not test the Lord, as some of them did. . . . And do not grumble, as some of them did" (1 Cor. 10:9-10).

My complaining was – finally and most honestly – a complaint against God: against Him for having let us get into such a mess. Had we not prayed about each decision we had made? Had we not really desired God's will to be done in our lives and our business? Let's face it, however much we might blame ourselves for some of the decisions we made, our particular circumstances did come directly from God's hand in the form of adverse weather. An ancient psalmist put it like this: "Lightning and hail, snow and clouds, stormy winds . . . do His bidding" (Ps. 148:8) — a pretty sobering thought when you find yourself trying to salvage a ruined crop.

I slowly began to realize that it is more honest and more direct to take our complaints right to God, the way Naomi does at the beginning of the Book of Ruth in the Old Testament. She doesn't say, "Elimelech and I made a terrible mistake." She doesn't say, "The folks back at home, or the government, or somebody out there is responsible." She says: "The Lord has afflicted me; the Almighty has brought misfortune upon me." Like Naomi, Job takes his case right to the highest court, traces the events of his life to the sovereign purposes of God: "The Lord gave and the Lord has taken away" — not, "The Lord gave and the Sabeans have taken away," or "The Lord gave and the firestorm has taken away." No, Job attributes his misfortune, as much as his good fortune, to a sovereign God — and only in that context is he able to say, "May the name of the Lord be praised" (Job 1:21).

Once I quit trying to "protect God" from my anger and frustration and confusion, I could quit blaming Cam and myself and my neighbor and the markets and the weather. I could say, *Lord — I don't get this. I don't know why You would let us be battered like this. But it's happening, so You must have allowed it for purposes I don't begin to understand. Help us to learn what You are trying to teach us. And P.S., Lord, please help us get out of this situation — soon.* I found something out in this struggle: when I quit blaming, Cam quit being defensive, and we began to have more constructive conversations, working together to formulate plans for our financial recovery. One of the really wonderful things about the hard months that long, cold winter after our business failed was that Cam and I actually had "quality time" together. More time to read the Scriptures and pray together than we had had for years. Time for a second cup of tea after supper. Time to pray—sometimes even at some length, in between the interruptions of four small children. The message that came through to us above all the others was very simple and just this: that God is, indeed, our Father. He gives only good gifts to His children—even when the wrapping is unattractive to our eyes.

A memory that sustained me was of my mother after she and my father were involved in a serious car accident. She had been released from the hospital, but her face was still swollen and misshapen, and she had a huge orange and purple bruise over her eyes. Mother could not move without pain, but she sat stiffly on a straight kitchen chair as I prepared a meal. Speaking with difficulty, since it hurt her even to catch a breath, she said in her quiet way, "It doesn't *feel* good, darling, but it must *be* good." It was an articulation of the kind of holding-on faith that my parents lived out before their family. And it's the kind of faith that helped Cam and me to know that behind the threatening clouds of economic reversals shone the sun of God's loving-kindness.

As we tried to sort things out, Cam would say, "The Lord knows, and the Lord knows I don't know." That too was a statement of faith. Just that one fact—that our Heavenly Father *knew*, both our situation and our real needs, material and spiritual—was something to hold onto until we could begin to discern His plans for us, "plans to give . . . hope and a future" (Jer. 29:11) expressed in our difficult circumstances.

Fending off bitterness—or rooting it out wherever we found it—was one kind of emotional and spiritual problem we had to cope with. Depression was another. The summer that we watched our business buckle under day by day, listening to the market reports as cattle prices slipped lower and lower, and then awakening to find our crops destroyed, we both fought depression. I found myself talking with God through sudden and frequent tears. I remember, especially, walking down the tree-lined lane of our rented property. When the poplar leaves were first bursting out of their sticky shells into little twin-kling valentine-shaped leaves, I struggled with having had to move our family into such a tiny house. I felt angry and help-less at our lack of money. I looked up through the new leaves to the sky and prayed, "Lord, none of this makes any sense to me at all. I only know one thing, and that is that *I love You.*" I made this declaration day after day, the spring colors of green and blue often blurred by my tears into a swimming green-blue underwater world where I felt I was drowning.

Then, as summer progressed, and things got worse, I would take the walk down the lane and look up into trees where the full-sized dark-green leaves blotted out the cloud-piled sky. And then I prayed another prayer: "Lord, it's even worse now. I don't know anything at all now." And then the little Sunday School hymn played itself out in my mind: *"Jesus loves me, this I know / For the Bible tells me so."* And I finished my prayer, "I don't know anything at all now, Lord . . . except that *You love me.*" And that is when I quit feeling like I was going to drown. I had found the bottom. Underneath all my grief and confusion there was the rocklike assurance of God's love. Underneath, after all, were the Everlasting Arms. And the love of God became a source, far greater than even our own great love for each other, on which we could draw as we learned to live on love.

Never, in any marriage, is there a time when loving support, deep sharing, and much prayer for a partner are more neces-sary than in such tough times. In easy times, it may be possi-ble to assume each other's love. In hard times, that love needs to be stated and reiterated. Not some kind of phony, artificial love, but love based on the discovery of strengths in each other. The wife can commend the husband's integrity and ap-preciate his concern for his family, while the husband can express appreciation for a wife's frugality and uncomplaining attitude. And love can thrive, for as Samuel Johnson pointed out, it is, after all, "a native of the rocks."

Later, as you pass through the experience together, you may both gain insights that will help you to keep the trauma from repeating itself. Under the guidance of the Holy Spirit and with all of His dovelike tenderness, a wife and a husband may minister to each other as they see weaknesses develop under the strain, or as they come to understand personal weakness that produced the strain in the first place. It becomes a matter of spiritual and personal survival to keep on "building up yourselves in your most holy faith" (Jude 20).

Preparing to Learn

As you commend each other's strengths and tenderly minister to each other's weaknesses, you can prepare yourselves to learn all that the Lord has for you in the experience of hardship. I can remember a morning when we were still trying to sort ourselves out after our debacle, when we suddenly understood: *There are two ways to respond to this experience. One is to withdraw, asking a whining, "Why?" and so shrivel in our souls. The other way is to reach out both hands for the experience . . . to "press against the pain" . . . to lean into the experience . . . and thus to learn all we can about this aspect of the human condition, and to grow.* We made up our minds that we would grow—no matter how it hurt. And Cam and I have found ourselves matured and quieted and corrected by the things we have faced together.

Of course, the days of hardship need not be ones of unbroken solemnity. In fact, heaven help the family who cannot laugh at themselves, laugh at their situation. (We do need to be careful here, for bitter laughter, laughter at each other's expense, and derisive laughter are all destructive. It is only the gentle laughter of people seeing life together, people who can see the ridiculousness of themselves or of their situation, that builds and helps.) The merciful gift of being able to laugh at ourselves—laugh with those we loved—was, for us, a healing agent.

Sharing the Load

Living on love means sharing the load. Sharing it in honest communication. Sharing it in recognition of individual

strengths and honest acknowledgment of one another's fail-
ures. Sharing it in the assessment of lessons learned and new
understandings gained. It also means sharing in the actual solution to the problem. It is not just enough to be honest with
each other and then fold your hands and stare at the ceiling,
waiting for a handout from the sky. God just does not work in
that way. In fact, the New Testament is explicit about the
necessity for working "with . . . [our] hands that [we] may
have something to share with those in need" (Eph. 4:28).

Let me share with you a letter my mother wrote to her four
children when she explained the terms of my grandfather's
will. It tells a story of how a whole family shared the load.

Grandpa and Grandma Woods were very hardworking
people with simple tastes and a contentment with their
lot in life—always grateful to the Lord for His provision
for them and their three children. Our home was furnished with plain, even rugged furniture, a few chintz
cushions for the seats of the hardwood chairs being the
only upholstery we knew. As we grew up and visited in
the homes of our friends, we children began to see the
new overstuffed Chesterfield suites which were really
quite new on the market and we began to pester our
parents for more elaborate things. Grandpa put a proposi-
tion to us: If we would help them save $1,000 as a cush-
ion for emergencies first, they would then add some better furniture to our home. I would have been about ten or
eleven years old, and my brothers were younger, so you
realize the only way we could help was by not asking for
things we didn't need.

We watched the bank account grow with real interest
and did reach our goal. However, about the same time as
we reached that goal, Grandpa lost his job with Canadian
Pacific Railways because of the economic crash in 1929.
He was able to get enough work that the emergency fund
was not depleted, but even we children understood that
luxuries were out. Then one day there was no more work

to be obtained, and Grandpa decided to try creating his own job. With the $1,000 he set up a business, which God honored and prospered far beyond any expectation so that Grandpa was able to support and educate his family and provide jobs for his two sons when jobs were very difficult for young men to find. Grandpa never went into debt for anything either in business or in the home. If there was not cash to pay for things, we did without, but we never lacked any of the necessities of life and Grandpa was never on "relief" or welfare as we know it now. As long as we lived at home there was no new furniture but later, when things improved after World War II, Grandpa and Grandma did enjoy comforts which we today think are necessities.

Grandpa was generous in his giving to the Lord's work, and I cannot tell you how grateful I am to the Lord and to Grandpa and Grandma, not merely for the money in the estate, but for the godly heritage they have given us — the example of frugal living combined with a deep desire to obey God's Word at any cost.

There, of course, may be times when it is necessary for a Christian family to accept welfare or unemployment insurance. Sometimes there is no other choice. But as people of God we should normally do everything in our power to find ways to earn the bread we eat and to repay the debts we have incurred.

Solving the Most Pressing Problems

Obviously, when we face a job loss or a business failure, the immediate problem is finding money for the day-to-day needs of a family. We had to find enough for our family's ongoing needs and work out a way to pay back debts. Job-hunting may be challenging at the best of times, but it is made doubly difficult when the job-seeker is feeling crushed and damaged in self-esteem. Finding something to do to meet immediate needs will be, for most families as it was for us, the biggest single step toward recovery. It may mean taking jobs beneath normal expectations. It will probably mean assessing the mutual job-finding resources of an entire family, with several members finding part-time work to help out. The spouse with the more marketable skills will have to "go for it," with support tasks redistributed according to the number of hours spent outside the home in earning.

For us, the first provision of income was a half-time job teaching high school French—a job in my field, rather than Cam's. Cam did the housekeeping along with winding down the business while I crammed to brush up my rusty French and taught. By spring, with much of the business attended to, Cam was able to take a short-term teaching job in another nearby town. Now the children had to help out too. Cam's parents offered to look after our two preschoolers while I taught—another provision. When the little ones found it hard to interrupt their play and pack up for the daily drive into town, I would explain the situation to them: "We're all helping each other just now. Grandma and Grandpa are helping by looking after you. Mom and Dad are helping each other by teaching—and now you can help me by getting on your coats without complaining." And so they did.

And so our hard winter resolved itself into spring, with clothes and groceries and car gas being paid for as we went along. We were blessed in having teaching jobs available; today, with down-sizing in corporations and government cutbacks, many professional people are finding it impossible to get relocated within their own area of training. Had there been no teaching jobs available, however, we would have considered whatever other options presented themselves. We talked seriously about the possibility that Cam might have to take a laboring job in the far north, in oil or in construction. And he would have done that, had not a job opened up for him close at hand. When economic reversal hits, we cannot afford to consider ourselves "above" any type of employment, regardless of previous training or job. We knew that we would take work— any kind of work we could find—to prevent ourselves from going further backward. And at the same time, we pruned our already lean budget to fit within our earning power.

You probably remember the Aesop fable about the frog in the cream jug. As I remember it from a grade-school reader, it goes something like this:

> One day, a frog fell into a jug that had been set outside to cool. At first, as the cool thick liquid closed around him, the frog thought, "Alas, all is lost. I shall drown in this cream." But then the frog thought to himself: *If I am to drown, it is better to drown struggling than simply lying here and sinking like a rock.* And so the frog began to kick and struggle with all of his strength. At first the cream just flowed around him, and then, just when he thought he had no more strength left for the struggle, he felt a little clot behind a back leg, and, with just one more burst of energy, the frog was standing on a little pat of butter which had formed as he had churned. And from that pat of butter, the frog was able to make one last leap — out of the cream jug and back into the pond.

That's how we felt by the end of the twelve months of struggle in which we reorganized our business affairs and began life again. We were weary from the struggle, but strong . . . and out of the cream jug.

Chapter Five

Stopping the Merry-Go-Round

"Want it? Charge it!" It's as easy as that—and, for many of us, as complicated.

I see the credit card companies on the campus where I teach, university students being encouraged to "establish their credit rating" by getting a card, and I remember how seductive credit cards were for us. As young marrieds, we found credit cards to be the magic key that unlocked all the things that more established people had. By means of credit buying, we could start living almost at the level our parents had achieved after many years of careful accumulation. And so, like most young people, we applied for credit cards: gas company cards, department store cards, feeling like we were joining the Club.

We were cautious in the use of those cards. One of the first uses we made of them was to outfit our tiny teacherage with simple, basic furniture. We were certainly not spendthrift, buying everything on sale and choosing what we felt was the best compromise between price and quality that we could make. Thinking back on the sum of our various expenditures, the figure seems ludicrously small. The department store whose card we used delivered the furniture to our new home in the village where we taught, and the monthly statement began to arrive in our mailbox. We were part of the economy. We belonged!

And making the payments posed no problem, since we were both earning a regular paycheck. Nonetheless, I remember the feeling of discouragement when, month after month, we made our payments, and yet the balance owing seemed to stay so high. It was our first taste of the fact that it was much easier to charge than to pay.

We quit charging, all at once, when we decided to go back to study together. Instead of spending, we saved. And the interest, instead of adding onto a balance payable account, started to be added to our credit balance in our savings account. We banked one paycheck each month and lived and made our credit payment from the other. It was exhilarating to pull in our belts and save for a goal. Our student years were lean even with the help we received from my parents in reduced rent on a basement suite and from Cam's folks in farm-grown vegetables. (One friend commented that we knew more ways to cook turnips than any couple he knew.) But we finished our studies debt-free.

Probably even sadder than students getting their own credit cards before they have landed their first jobs is the debt many young people accumulate before ever getting to those jobs. The ball and chain of loan repayments that many young people have to drag through the first decade of employment makes me feel sad and angry. Angry that it is necessary for students to mortgage their futures for their education; sad that the standard of living for students has become so high that, for most students, extensive borrowing is the only way to sustain it. Especially with the uncertainty that there will be a job immediately upon graduation—at least a job commensurate with one's training and expectations—it might be better to "live lean." (OK, so skip the turnips! But, after all, learning frugality early may be the best part of an education for the years ahead!) Some should consider taking a year out from their studies to save ahead rather than incurring large student loans—loans which will have to be paid off at the low end of their earning power while they are trying to establish a home and start a family.

A New Start

With studies behind us for the time being, we celebrated life by making a down payment on a new car, buying a green canvas tent, and setting out on a cross-country camping trip. And then we entered consumer life in earnest. Cam was the principal of a school, and his income was about the same as our combined salaries had been prior to our return to the university. I was expecting our first child and had time to turn the pages of the fat catalogs which, for people in rural areas like ours, served as department stores. And, with my shiny new credit cards, I was able to charge the things we needed. I'm sure that everything I bought was quite legitimate and defensible. I know I never shopped frivolously. But I remember the sudden shock and panic that struck me when, after the delight of numbers of little parcels arriving in the mail, the statements followed. I could hardly imagine that the "few little things" I had bought had pushed the balance on our two accounts to a combined $300. The other shock came over the next few months. Do you know how long it takes to reduce a balance of $300 at the minimum monthly payment of $12? Forever. At least, it seems that long. Especially if you happen to add a thing or two to that account as you go along.

I was learning that the exciting consumer concept of revolving credit was a merry-go-round with the music stuck in an endless, mindless ditty of "buy now, and pay and pay and pay." It was a merry-go-round that never had to stop at all. And every ad I read, every page of every catalog, every visit to the department stores in the city, and every mailing "to preferred credit customers" was designed to flatter me with the idea that somehow I was a notch above the rest of the world because I held a red, white, or blue credit card for a given store.

Then we went farming. And when big spending times of the year came around—like snowsuit-time or Christmas—and there simply was no money because the grain was still not marketed, the charge cards came in handy again. I could rattle off those tempting numbers and, after dictating my order, say nonchalantly, "Just charge it to our account." I knew my numbers by heart. And I was treated with the deference given to regular charge customers. The balances began to build up again.

Worst of all, the monthly statements had a way of coming out to coincide with the time when most average people were bringing home their paychecks. But we had no paycheck. Just those big, tantalizing lump sums that came with shipping a load of pigs or selling a bin of grain—those big checks that melted away as we paid outstanding bills to the businesses that had delivered our gas, stockpiled our fertilizer, or sold us seed. It was hard to scratch up enough, on a month-to-month basis, to pay even the minimum payments on those charge accounts. And if there's one thing I cannot face, it's a dunner: "We hope that your failure to make a payment last month was an oversight. However, terms of our credit agreement with you stipulate that if we do not receive your payment of _____ by _____, we shall _____." Those notes devastated me. Not that we were defaulting in any long-term way. As soon as there was money, we paid the back payment and one or two in advance. We simply limped from lump to lump. And between times, I would find myself having to charge something or other, pushing up that balance once again.

It finally dawned on me that the whole principle of the revolving credit system was that you should never get a balance paid off. You should always have a balance, pay interest on it, pay off some and add on some. And about the same time, it dawned on me that it was those monthly accounts that made me most unhappy and most discontent. They were the things that precipitated those "Why can't we live like normal people?" discussions with Cam which cheered him so. Combining each month—with fiendish regularity—with those days when I felt mad at the world in general—those bills made month ends very blue.

Taking Charge
One year I finally made the big decision: there was no way that I was going to charge one thing for Christmas. Not one little thing. Cam and I liked to have great Christmas gifts for the kids. But when we noticed that we were still paying for each

Christmas deep into the following year, we made our decision firm. "No matter how little we can buy, we're going to pay cash for Christmas gifts this year." Now, that may sound only reasonable to you, but for us it was a new departure, a new beginning. We paid cash for Christmas, trimming the gift list, withdrawing from drawing names, and shopping as thriftily as we could. And on that Christmas Day, every gift that was opened was prepaid. The only day nicer than December 25 was January 25, when there were no additional charges on those revolving accounts of ours. And February 25. And March 25. Less pressure, less depression, fewer arguments.

That experiment prepared us to take action when several years later, we found that our cattle-feeding company was completely broke. We took what little money we had in the bank and paid all of our charge accounts: gas accounts, department store accounts, and the grocery account. It left us flat. But from that day we decided that during this time of financial exigency, either the Lord would supply us with cash or we would not buy. That applied right down to the next loaf of bread we needed for school lunches. We learned to pray, "Give us this day our daily bread." And He did. There was often very little extra. Cam used to say, "You know, our cupboards would make Mother Hubbard's look like a supermarket." But there was always enough—for that day, at least.

I remember well a week when all our food supplies were at an all-time low. But we had no money. None at all. So we took our request to the Lord in prayer. The last day of the week, the mail contained two small checks: one a reprint fee for an article of mine, the other a small overpayment refund for Cam. The total was no staggering amount, but we went shopping. We shopped with all the joy I used to know as a little girl with a dime to spend in Woolworth's. We shopped selectively. We picked things up, adding up the total in our heads as we went, and then pushed the cart back and returned some of the things to the shelves. And when we went home, we had all that we needed. Plus joy and gratitude.

The greatest delight, besides that of having no more month-end pressures when month ends brought so little of anything else, was the pleasure of being freed from the need to buy. I could look at one of those ads reading, "Go Ahead! Charge It!" and feel more nausea than desire. I had the happy feeling that month by month, despite inflation, I was at least not having to pay those scarcely perceptible little service charges and exorbitant interest rates that are normal on credit-card accounts.

I noticed something else too. Without those credit cards in my purse, I was free to shop. I mean, really shop. I didn't have to go to the stores where I was a gilt-edged, card-carrying member. I could go anywhere for the best values. I noticed it most of all when buying gas. As long as I had a particular company's card in my purse, all I looked for was a service station sporting the right color and shape of sign, and wheeled in for gas. Without those little bits of plastic, I read, instead, the price-per-gallon signs, and bought where the price was right.

Getting off the credit merry-go-round was just part of our overall "face-the-facts" policy. Not that using a charge card is wrong for everyone. Many people are able to control their spending well enough to pay every credit balance in full. But allowing yourself to buy things you cannot afford today, in the hope that you will be able to afford them — plus interest — next month, is living a myth. So is it when you think that buying things in easy monthly payments is really easy. It's not. Without those plastic crutches, I could look at our bank balance and decide whether I could afford to buy or not. Some years, it has been mostly not. And yet, the goodness of the Lord's provision is unforgettable.

Steps to Controlled Credit
If you are on the credit-card trip and want to get off, here are some tips. First of all, in order to get the charge accounts paid, you need to impose a period of several months of real austerity on yourself, buying only absolute necessities like groceries. If you have a regular income, budget to pay off the accounts in an orderly way as fast as you can. And put nothing — but noth-

ing—more on that account. "I can hardly wait," a friend of mine told me. "In a couple of months, we should have all our accounts paid off. Then we're going to only buy with cash." And then she went to the city with her charge cards in her purse. The temptation was too much as she browsed in the big stores. "It all came to only $250," she told me as she showed me her purchases. "I charged it." Six months later we each drank a Coke as we chatted. "That miserable charge account is right up there again," she sighed. "And it all started that time I charged those clothes."

The way to stop the merry-go-round is to put those credit cards in some safe and nonpilferable place—anywhere but your purse. If you do not want to destroy them yet, store them in an envelope, deep in a file, or better yet, in a safety deposit box. That will make them hard to grab when your fingers get the dial-an-order itch. If you must make purchases while you are trying to reduce your charge accounts, pay cash. And chisel away at the balances you owe as fast as you can. Then, when the accounts are down to a zero balance and you get that lovely letter, reading, "We are pleased with the excellent way in which you have handled your credit. Please feel free to use your credit card at any time"—and the follow-up one which tells you what a valued customer you are and how they yearn to send you a bill once more—forget it. It's not real love.

Living in the Real World

Now, at last, you can begin to live in the real world. And despite all the invitations to use credit as though money will somehow "happen along" later, we all know that everyone, from governments to individuals, has to face reentry into the reality of economics: for goods received, value must be given. And the easiest, surest, most direct way to be sure that you can give value for goods received is to pay as you go—an idea so old-fashioned as to be positively avant-garde.

Living in this real world, you will exercise restraint, and begin the lifelong learning process of disciplining your heart to contentment. As you learn how to distinguish between wants and needs, you will no longer be driven by advertising. "And my God will meet all your needs" is God's promise to His children, backed by "His glorious riches in Christ Jesus" (Phil. 4:19). But nowhere, *not anywhere,* in Scripture does God invite us to help ourselves to everything we want. In fact, we are continually warned to beware of buying into a value system that is driven by "the cravings of sinful man, the lust of his [or her] eyes and the boasting of what he [or she] has and does" (1 John 2:16). You might try analyzing the advertisements in a current magazine or on an evening of television by those three motivational phrases. They still represent the fundamental drives behind our desire to buy and consume beyond our real needs. Isn't that why advertisers pay huge sums to TV networks and big money to clever makers of commercials — to get you to buy?

In our lean years, I learned a way I still use to winnow out "needs" from "wants." Once in awhile, I make a list of all the things that I would like to have that are badgering away at my brain — usually on a back page of the coil notebook I call my "journal." Just getting them out of my head and onto paper helps clear my head. Often I can immediately distinguish between bubbles, baubles, and needs. A few days later many of the items on it do not seem quite so pressing as they did when I wrote them down. Now I can quite deliberately separate the items into several lists: In "List A" I can place items which fulfill physical needs — clothes suitable to the climate in which we live; warm and adequate housing; nutritious food for ourselves and our families; some mode of transportation — an essential need unless you live where public transportation can get you where you have to go. In "List B" I prioritize items which fulfill social needs — like gifts to be purchased or supplies for a celebration. In "List C" I can list items which are related to production: from the tape recorder or word processor that would help me get my work done to the combine we need to buy for farming. Items which do not fit into any of these lists, I can relegate to "List D" — a wish list of "someday-maybe" things which are attractive and legitimate but not essential at this time.

"List A" items are top priority items—needs to be met as soon as and to the extent that we can afford. "List B" items may have to be scaled down to fit the budget—but they too need to be looked after. "List C" items are business decisions which need to be looked at in terms of productive capability. If they will not directly affect production, they will have to wait for cash on hand; if they will really increase earning capability, they may be capital expenditures necessary to getting on with our work, something we might have to arrange a short-term loan for.

"List D" items—the "someday-maybe" ones—tend to lose their urgency when they get separated from more pressing needs. I can look at them and ask some other questions, like, "Is this an item that I might want to put in a garage sale a few years from now?"

I can now go back through those lists and number them in order of priority—and on the basis of that, make wise spending decisions.

Using Credit Wisely

I have been talking about getting off the endless merry-go-round of credit for consumable items. There are, of course, other kinds of completely legitimate credit which I am sure God intends for Christians to use wisely and well. Very few families could have a home if they had to pay cash for it. Very few could start a business. And most people would not even be able to drive a car. Christian thinkers have drawn a distinction between borrowing for consumable items (debt) and borrowing for capital items (investment). This difference is set forth memorably in Robert Schuller's account of how his banker explained to him the meaning of debt:

> When you borrow money for coal, you are going into debt. The coal will be burned. When it is gone, if you are unable to pay your loan, there is nothing you can sell to pay us back. When you borrow money for coal,

or food, or the light bill, or the water bill, you are spending money that is gone forever. This is real debt.

But the banker went on to explain:

> If you want to borrow money to buy a car or a house, we will lend you money. Then you are not going into debt; you are going into the investment business. . . . If you borrow money to buy a store and you borrow money for salable goods to put on the shelves, you are not in debt. You are in business.[1]

Yet, here again, a clear head, an open Bible, a good banker, and a clear line of communication between you and your mate are necessary to be sure that you are using credit instead of it using you. In our farming company, the money we borrowed was very legitimate and used for the purposes of production. Yet, we still borrowed ourselves into very serious economic problems. An article in *Changing Times,* the Kiplinger Magazine, suggests "one safety rule is never to owe more at any one time than you can repay within twelve months at your current rate of payments," making, of course, exceptions for large, long-term loans such as those for homes.[2] Another rule of thumb would be never to borrow more than you have fixed assets to cover. Thus, if you found yourself unable to meet current obligations, you would be able to sell assets and cover your indebtedness.

Friends of ours recently recounted to us that when their insurance agent came to review their coverage, they decided to have him help them draw up a net worth statement. They listed all of their assets in one column, and totaled them; all of their liabilities were listed in a second column and totaled. When the insurance man subtracted the total liabilities from their total assets, he looked up at them, obviously surprised. They had a substantial surplus of assets. "You know," the insurance salesman told them, "there are very few couples today who have a positive net worth. When I work this out for most people, we find they actually owe more than they own."

When You Cannot Pay

Another problem remains to be discussed in this credit-abundant society. What about credit debts which you have at the moment that your business goes sour? Or you lose your job? Or illness destroys your earning power while adding burdens?

A Christian cannot just walk away from debt. His word is pledged, and he must acknowledge his obligations. But to avoid an unpleasant outcome, the best route is simply to be honest and open. Go to your creditors personally, or write them a letter. Explain the situation and ask for time in which to reorganize your finances. Suggest a time when you will be able to begin to reduce the debt, if that time can be foreseen. Let them know your fiscal condition, and assure them that you are serious about repaying the obligation. If you are straightforward and honest, if you have pared down your lifestyle to an extremely modest standard so that you are credible, if you continue to keep in touch and make even token payments of good faith, then your creditors will be remarkably patient as you attempt to get your business affairs straightened out.

I once worked as a typist in collection agencies. In one office, I typed envelopes while at ten or twelve desks in the same large room men sat and dialed persons whose debts were considered "bad" and had been turned over to them for collection. The men yelled and threatened and bullied, and I felt the horror of how it must feel to be at the other end of such a call. But creditors do not like turning accounts over to collection agencies, since they lose a percentage of every payment collected. Despite financial problems, we have found that honesty with our creditors, restraint in our personal living, and systematic planning for repayment of what seemed to us to be staggering debts have resulted in fair and courteous treatment from those to whom we have owed money. We rejected bankruptcy as a means of avoiding debt obligations, even though our debts had been incurred by a limited company. And, through the goodness of the Lord and the patience of our creditors, we have been able to pay back all that we owed. It is a good feeling—a mixture of gratitude and relief.

So, do we still use credit? Yes, of course. But very cautiously, never forgetting the sick feeling of finding debt out of control. We do use credit cards to avoid having to carry around a lot of cash, but we are still aware of how easy it is to overspend with plastic. Paying the full balance every month keeps us from getting back on the buy-now and pay-forever merry-go-round we remember too well. Our businesses run on operating credit which allows us to seed a crop in the spring and harvest it in the fall, or take time off from my teaching or speaking to write a book, and yet keep a relatively stable cash flow. And although we have retired much of our capitalization debt, we are still making payments on long-term loans for land and machinery.

We remember now how, on our honeymoon, we went with friends to an exhibition ground where we went through the exhilaration and terror of the enormous roller coaster, bounced on the trampolines, and survived some other rides. Then we all went out together for Alka-Seltzer. That's how the memory of overextended credit feels to us; we're a bit squeamish, even yet; we get sick at the thought of it ever getting out of control. But we are off the roller coaster, for good.

Chapter Six

Basic Needs I: Sharing the Good Things

We are not a family big on playing board games. Not that there is anything wrong with them; we have admired families that have made more time for game-playing. Maybe our lack of interest has been because life itself has sometimes seemed like a complicated and frustrating enough board game. I remember how, in the midst of our financial reversal, I could not stand playing games where some flick of the wrist might mean you got a message: "Return to Start." We were in the process of doing that, and it was no fun. Or maybe our lack of interest in games is because, when we get together with others, we would rather have a conversation than total up points. Or maybe it is nothing more or less than pure pragmatics: as a family we found other means of entertainment simply because we could not afford to purchase every new game that came along. At any rate, we have a sparse collection of games in our games cupboard.

But although our choice of games was not big, we did develop a tradition: at least once during the Christmas holidays, we would sit down and play a game of Monopoly with Mitchell, our youngest son, who had already demonstrated his entrepreneurial instincts by the time he was six and was caring for the seven little weanling pigs his sow had birthed. He still remembers (with some vexation) how I used to lay aside 10 percent of any payout I received and play it on a second, imaginary game board on which I could buy food for hungry kids, place Bibles in people's hands in their own languages, develop literacy and agricultural programs, and support missionaries in church-planting. And when the end of the game came (admittedly, a bit sooner than it might have had I not pulled so much play money out of circulation), I usually not only owned Park Avenue but also had made an imagined difference somewhere, in someone's life.

Playing Monopoly so subversively was a lighthearted but natural way in which to express one of our fundamental beliefs: the conviction that giving is not something one does once in awhile, but a basic need, something that we do as a part of our economic existence.

The Need to Give

No matter how hard-pressed we have been, we have found that one of our first and most basic needs is the need to share in the "shalom" or well-being of others. Since from our Christian perspective, that well-being is complex and includes the physical, emotional, intellectual, and spiritual needs of others, the range of ways in which we are able to give is also wide and complex. In concentric circles of caring, beginning with our own family circle and widening out to our church family and community and then to the larger community, we have tried to keep aware of others as well as of our own needs.

Our gifts of money have been, as such have always been seen to be, earthly tokens of an essentially spiritual commitment: our lives themselves are gifts from God; all that we have and are we have given — or are in the daily process of learning how to give — back to the Giver. Monetary gifts remind us of that underlying commitment. And, as C.S. Lewis puts it, "If our charities do not at all pinch or hamper us, I should say they are too small."[1]

Because giving meets two basic needs in our own lives — our need to affirm "who we are" by reminding ourselves of "whose we are" as well as our need to live in connection with other needy human beings in order to keep our own needs in perspective — we have found it works best to plan our giving and do it first. Whenever we have tried to save a little through-out the month in order to give, we have found that our own needs have overwhelmed our urge to give. But when we have given our love-gifts first, we have found that somehow there has been enough for the month ahead. I am not sure that I know *how* that works — but I know *that* it works.

Biblical Principles of Giving

Giving as a basic mark of discipleship is stressed throughout the New Testament. Jesus looked out at a hungry crowd and laid the responsibility for the welfare of the people directly on the shoulders of His disciples — the very people who had given up their means of earning a living to follow Him: "You give them something to eat" (Matt. 14:16). The disciples were, apparently, stunned at the command. They did the mental cal-culations and felt their empty purses. And they learned that, if they were to fulfill their Lord's command, they would have to rely on their Lord's resources.

Paul continues the theme of openhanded giving, inviting the Christian believers at Philippi to give not only to meet his needs, but to meet their own need of obedient giving. (You can follow his discussion of this important theme in Philippians 4:10-20.) Giving, Paul argues, produces lasting spiritual benefit in the lives of the givers.

Of course, giving is not a novel theme in the New Testa-ment. It is simply an enlargement of a theme already devel-oped in the Old Testament. Because God is love, throughout history those who have understood His revelation of Himself have understood the obligation of sharing the good things of life with others. The tradition of giving as a moral responsibil-ity can be traced back as far as to Job. In defending his righ-teous conduct, Job recounts acts of charity which he sees to be both social and spiritual obligations:

> If I have denied the desires of the poor or let the eyes
> of the widow grow weary,

> if I have kept my bread to myself,
>   not sharing it with the fatherless. . . .
> if I have seen anyone perishing for
>   lack of clothing,
>   or a needy man without a garment,
> and his heart did not bless me
>   for warming him with the fleece from my sheep
> . . . then let my arm fall from the shoulder,
>   let it be broken off at the joint.
> For I dreaded destruction from God,
>   and for fear of His splendor I could not do
>   such things (Job 31:16-23).

Job's sense of social obligation is rooted in his fear of the Lord: his sense that he lives out his life in the presence of One whose holiness demands that His creatures take responsibility for each other.

Yet, Job was still yearning for "Someone" to come: "If only there were someone to arbitrate between us, to lay his hand upon us both, someone to remove God's rod from me" (Job 9:33-34). That "Someone" has come in the person of the Lord Jesus Christ. The New Testament believer, motivated by love for the One who "though He was rich, yet for [our] sakes He became poor, so that [we] through His poverty might become rich" (2 Cor. 8:9) should surely not be less socially responsible than was Job. In glad and loving response to Jesus' self-giving, we *need* to give.

We need to give, and not only because there are physical needs which must be met by our giving. Our "headline news" awareness of those needs make us painfully aware of them, so painfully aware, in fact, that sometimes we become anesthetized, inured by visual familiarity to so much suffering. We need to give also because in giving we share in "the grace of our Lord Jesus Christ." In giving, in sharing in His gracious self-giving, we begin to learn a little of what it is to be Christlike — the lifetime goal of any believer. After all, the One who Jesus invites us to call "Father" is, at heart, the Great Giver (as

Jesus teaches in Matthew 5:43-48, and James reiterates in James 1:16-18).

And as *forgiving others* seems to be necessary to clear a channel through which God's forgiveness can reach us (Matt. 6:14-15), so *giving to others* seems to operate to clear a channel through which we can receive God's physical provision for our needs. It is not that we give more in order to receive more — but that we give something in order to open the way for the provision of "our daily bread." We do not give away the money the Lord has given us for our mortgage payment and expect to get double the amount in the mail the next day. We budget our incomes and discipline ourselves to give, proportionate to what God entrusts to us for our stewardship, in accordance with clear New Testament principles and guidelines. These principles cover matters of *motivation* for giving, the *measure* of our giving, and the *method* of our giving.

1. *Motivation.* The motivation of love and obedience that prompts Christian giving will always be a mystery to those on the outside looking in. No matter how sophisticated and professional our fund-raising appeals may become, the secret of lifelong generous giving that combines discipline with joy will always be found, as it was in the generous, poverty-stricken Christians of the opening decades of the history of the church, in people's giving of themselves "first to the Lord and then to [others]" (2 Cor. 8:1-5). Other appeals — whether based on sentimental response to the pathos of others' needs or on the very human desire to be part of some spectacular project or program may result in spasms of philanthropy, but will never produce steady, sustained giving.

The motivation for Christian "charity" is not primarily in the need of others — although the Christian is aware of those needs and seeks to meet them. Even less is it in any idea that God needs our gifts in order to accomplish His will. We do not give because God needs our money. We give because He invites us to share in His goodness. We give because we live in relationship with a God who is a Giver. We give because in giving we grow in our capacity to know and love Him. We give because giving is the natural, glad response of love and thanksgiving for God's goodness to us. We are not primarily motivated by the needs we see, real and pressing as they are. Rather, we first decide to give out of love to God, and then we find the needs that our gifts might best address.

There have been times when we have been able to give more, and times when we have been able to give less. There have been times when we could give with the delight of skimming cream off the rich milk of God's goodness, and times when the milk was so thin it was blue — and we offered from our skim milk. We have been assured from Scripture that God was pleased to accept and bless our gifts, whether they came from our prosperity or from our poverty.

2. *Measure.* How much should we give? These days, in a reaction against legalism, we are in danger of losing touch with our deep traditions and history. The church for centuries held out the measure or norm of the tithe: one-tenth of all that is entrusted to us is to be returned to God as a matter of course.

And in doing that, the church was simply extending a deep and ancient practice from the Old Testament. By the end of the Old Testament, the tithe was so clearly understood as a principle that to withhold it could be declared to be a form of theft. In the dialogue between God and His people in the Book of Malachi, God asks: "Will a man rob God? Yet you rob Me." The people of God reply, "How do we rob You?" And God's answer is clear: "In tithes and offerings" (Mal. 3:7-8). If the tithe was an appropriate standard of giving for the Old Testament, the New Testament standard would surely be to give at least as much as the tithe — surely not less than the tithe. Jesus, fulfilling the spirit of the Old Testament Law in His relationship with God and with others, sets the standard of total giving in His self-emptying.

For me, the tithe continues to make sense as the foundational principle of systematic giving. It seems to me to be a principle which, since it was clearly practiced long before the giving of the Mosaic Law, is still "in force" now, after the fulfillment of the Mosaic Law by our Lord Jesus Christ. Abraham, we read, tithed to Melchizedek, king and priest (as reported in Genesis 14:18 and commented on in Hebrews 7). Abraham seems to have tithed not because tithing was a law, but apparently because it was a principle of giving that had already been established by tradition. We, who claim "faithful Abraham" as a spiritual ancestor, should surely give as faithfully in the name of and for the advancement of the kingdom of our High Priest and King, Jesus Christ.

Jacob is another of the patriarchs who demonstrates that tithing is not just a rule of law. He made a business deal with God:

> If God will be with me and will watch over me on this journey I am taking and will give me food to eat and clothes to wear so that I return safely to my father's house, then the Lord will be my God . . . and of all that You give me I will give You a tenth (Gen. 28:20-22).

And even though the cheating, self-interested Jacob still had a long way to go before he would return to that place of covenant to be renamed (Gen. 35:9), the deal he made reinforces the point that the tithe is not just some sort of legal obligation, but deeply rooted in a tradition. *The tithe is paid by those who live out their lives by faith in an unseen God.*

So it seems to me that it is quite compatible with Scripture to see the tithe as the basic unit of giving—rooted in pre-Mosaic Law relationships of God and His people, a standard by which giving less than the tithe is judged to be simple robbery, and a principle echoed in the New Testament in the principle of proportional giving. "On the first day of every week, each one of you should set aside a sum of money *in keeping with his [or her] income*" (1 Cor. 16:2, emphasis added). Returning to God 10 percent of the total income that has been entrusted to us is a way to be sure that our giving is proportional to our prosperity.

If tithing is the foundational principle of giving—the floor under our giving—then we might consider that, as my father used to put it, "Giving starts where tithing leaves off." And I can remember an envelope on my parents' dresser ready for the offering labeled with my father's precise cursive — "Lord's Money." That envelope was the first thing attended to when the monthly paycheck came. Everything else came after that.

Giving, then, represents digging a bit deeper or reaching a bit higher. For some in extreme duress, the tithe may be all that can be returned to the Lord. For others, the tithe will be a small portion of what can be spared. For people who carry a heavy debt load, a matter of integrity is involved. After they have tithed, they must give primary attention to the repaying of contracted obligations. God cannot be honored by Christians who default on debts or postpone repayment in order to respond to some need. (And, by the way, that's just one more good reason to keep off the credit merry-go-round. If you don't have those monthly statements to pay, you may be able to cinch in your belt and give generously to a need that the Lord brings to your attention.) I find most challenging a concept of "needs limitation" in which Christian families accept a fixed figure at which they can live simply and modestly but without undue pressure. They adjust that figure to the annual rise in the cost of living, and then, rather than expanding their needs to meet their income, they expand their giving to invest the balance of their income for the glory of God. All income over and above the fixed ceiling can be given to the Lord. Another interesting idea is Ronald J. Sider's modest proposal for a graduated tithe. He says in an article in *Theology, News and Notes:*

> How about a graduated or sliding scale for our giving? We could sit down and carefully and honestly figure out what we would need to live for a year in reasonable comfort, but without some of the luxuries . . . plus a certain amount for each child. . . . We would give a tithe on the basic amount. . . . Then, on the first $1,000 over the basic amount, we would give 15 percent to the Lord's work; on the next $1,000, we would give 20 percent.[2]

And so on. It's another workable plan for people who are serious about giving by God's standard.

3. *Method.* So, you've got your tithes and offerings figured out. Or you have written the amount on a check. Now, just to whom should you make that amount payable? It would be simple, wouldn't it, if we could just write "God" on the payable line and let Him take it from there. But God uses earthly clearinghouses. And the responsibility of stewardship comes into the picture again. God does not rule out our intelligence or our responsibility when it comes to giving. No merit exists in mindless, purposeless giving of our tithes and offerings as we are blown about by every breeze of fervent appeal.

We need to give systematically, prayerfully, and thoughtfully if we are to be considered faithful stewards. There are three main areas to which our giving will be directed under the leading of the Holy Spirit and the teaching of the Word of God:

• *Our local church.* Every local fellowship of believers has material obligations which require its support. The first concern is paying the pastor: "Anyone who receives instruction in the Word must share all good things with his instructor" (Gal. 6:6). The gaunt and starving preacher should exist only among gaunt and starving people. God's Word is clear about the responsibility of God's people to attend carefully to the physical needs of the one who labors for their spiritual benefit. A minister should live at the average standard of living of his parishioners, neither higher nor lower. If all tithes (as distinct from offerings) were given to the local church, and half of them were used to support the general church budget, building maintenance, and programs, the other half of the tithes of every twenty families could support a minister at a wage representing an exact average of their incomes. It is something to think about, although simplistic, perhaps, in terms of large churches with huge buildings, many staff members, and multitudinous programs. Yet the principle remains: a lion's share of our giving, at least of our tithing, needs to be channeled into supporting our local church. As a pastor of mine once put it: "You pay for your groceries at the store where you buy them — not at some other store down the street. So with your giving. You give your tithes where you and your family are getting the bread of life." If you find yourself unable to support the programs and ministries of the church you attend with your tithes, perhaps you should look for another fellowship whose message or method you can endorse more wholeheartedly, and to which you can give not only your time but also your tithe.

• *Giving to further the proclamation of the Gospel.* This involves looking out beyond the local, community programs of your own church, and seeing the need for worldwide evangelism. It should be a priority item on every Christian's "gift list." If your church or denomination has a strong missionary program, you may direct your gifts through that channel. You might also like to save some of your offerings for more personal giving. Many missionaries are proclaiming the Gospel of Jesus Christ while being supported solely by the monthly gifts of friends at home. And when you know such a "faith missionary" personally, or feel moved by the Spirit of God to support the work of one, you will experience that rare kind of joy that comes from many years of participation — by prayer and gifts — in another's ministry.

To me the most important aspect of this kind of sharing is that it helps you to remember that missionary friend on a regular basis. Your giving has a face on it. And, as Jesus pointed out, "Where your treasure is, there will your heart be also" (Matt. 6:21). The partnership which begins with giving matures into a prayer fellowship which means that you enter personally into the work of evangelism. Thus, even though your share of a missionary's support may be miniscule, those few dollars a month represent an investment of yourself in the missionary's work. Your family can join in the excitement of letters exchanged and furlough-time visits, and all of you will be enriched by this kind of fellowship.

Another kind of special love relationship is in supporting an indigenous pastor or evangelist. Here, there is a multiplication of your dollars in supporting people who already know the languages and cultures in which they seek to work, and whose monetary needs are much lower than even the most frugal North American.

• *Physical needs of the hungry and suffering.* This is a third kind of need to which Christian giving is directed. Giving to relieve the hungry, the destitute, the victims of catastrophe should not supplant our giving to the local church or to the cause of world evangelism. But in these days we should be giving more, over and above our tithes and regular offerings whenever possible, as we recognize our responsibility to relieve human suffering wherever we can. There are excellent Christ-centered and love-motivated organizations handling relief funds skillfully that we can give to in the loving Spirit of Christ.

Day after day, as we flip the pages of our magazines and turn on our television sets, we find ourselves looking into the eyes of hunger-haunted little ones, children of poverty, children of disease. And the ache becomes so great that we have to anesthetize ourselves. Or respond. Jesus' story of the sheep and goats in the great Judgment Day should be reread and restudied for its social implications today (Matt. 25:31-46). We will, as nations, be judged for our generosity—or lack of it—to those in need. And if as nations, then surely as individuals we will have to give account for our responsiveness. Some of us will have much to give; some, very little. But all of us can give, remembering that God measures our giving not in terms of how much we give, but rather, in terms of how much we keep for ourselves.

John Wesley, pondering the dilemma of the link between righteousness and riches, made a suggestion which is still valid today:

Is there no way to prevent this continued decay of pure religion? We ought not to prevent people from being diligent and frugal; we must exhort all Christians to gain all they can and save all they can, that is, in effect, to grow rich. What way can we take that our money-

making may not sink us to the nethermost hell? There
is one way.... *If those who gain all they can and save
all they can will also give all they can, then, the more they
will grow in grace and the more treasure they will lay up
in heaven.*"[3]

Chapter Seven

Basic Needs II: Food and Clothing

Food

In the midst of our financial stress, I had a long period of illness leading up to major surgery. As I lay in a hospital bed watching the drip of the intravenous tube, I thought about how much time I would save in my life if we all just ate intravenously all the time. Just think, no time spent in food preparation or clean-up. I could just sit at my typewriter all day, every day, and eat through my hand! Of course, the idea was ludicrous. For food is very much a part of our lives, and you have to be pretty sick before another arrangement for nourishment looks better than sitting down together to a meal.

In personal spending, food takes one of the major chunks of our income — in North America, something between 18 and 25 percent of disposable income, depending on the level of income. Of course, in many countries of the world, the percentage of earned income spent on food is much higher — in some countries, people have to spend up to 80 percent of what is earned just to eat.[1]

And in daily living, as any homemaker knows, food demands a good deal of our time and attention. Growing it, shopping for it, storing it, preparing it, serving it, cleaning up after it: it all takes time.

There's nothing wrong with that, of course. But anything that demands such a large part of our income and our daily energy surely needs to be thought through carefully. We need to have healthy, sane attitudes toward food so that we can be good custodians of our food dollars, of the time we spend on, with, and over food, and ultimately, of the bodies we are responsible for nurturing.

Nutrition and Celebration

Food, of course, is more than merely a matter of nutrition— although that is its primary significance. We eat in order to live, and the nutritional role of food in the shaping of healthy bodies and minds is a matter of such importance that we really cannot just leave it to chance. We need to be informed and knowledgeable about food and nutrition.

But, over and above nutrition, food serves a secondary but also important role in our lives as an element of celebration. Our need for nutrition is undeniable; it is a physical requisite. But our need for celebration is an emotional, social, and spiritual aspect of life which we cannot neglect, either. And food serves as a center or focal point of celebration not only at special festive seasons—Thanksgiving, Christmas, Easter in our Western Christian tradition—but also daily as we gather as families for a shared meal, celebrating the provision of "our daily bread."

It seems a particularly perverse turn of events that in our Western societies, with access to great quantities of food, we should have lost sight of the value of food in both of its aspects: so many of our meals are haphazard events, taken hastily and with little planning from package to plate and eaten while plumped in individualized isolation in front of the television.

A period of real hardship probably had the beneficial effect for us of making us really notice what we had always before taken for granted: The gift of provision on a daily basis as a gift to be celebrated together. I can remember the joy we shared together in churning butter in a glass "Daisy churn," the children taking turns as the wooden paddles at first moved easily in the milk and then gradually became harder and harder to turn. Cam usually had to take over before we reached the exciting "voilà" moment when, suddenly, we had butter. I remember too the joy of receiving a small check for an article in the mail just in time for Saturday shopping.

I especially remember a Saturday when we had company coming for supper. We had home-churned butter for our home-baked bread. We had home-grown beef and home-hoed potatoes. But what could we have for dessert? Sugar prices had soared that winter as our income had plummeted, and I was eking out a five-pound bag by teaspoonfuls. As a family, we had quit having desserts with regular meals. But as I selected a few groceries at the village store, I glanced up to see the proprietor's wife blocking my way, holding a big bag of oranges. "Could you use these?" she asked. "They won't keep over the weekend." Sliced oranges, topped with fresh whipped cream, made our dessert that night. Our guests were charmed: such simplicity! such originality!

Blessedly, we had four little children to keep our mealtimes celebratory—sometimes uproariously so. We needed the buoyancy and joy of the children, and fed on their laughter and chatter and sense of the ridiculous even as they fed on the food we had prepared. For us, the evening meal each day became a central celebration of life and of each other.

I am not, of course, suggesting that every evening meal looked like one of those mouth-watering illustrations in the women's magazines. Stew or homemade soup and a thousand variations on hamburger casseroles and skillets were staples. Nor am I suggesting that every supper was an idyll of family sweetness and light. We had lots of salt and vinegar in our relationships too. But meals were planned; and we did sit down together to eat them. And after the food had disappeared into six healthy appetites, we asked for another disappearing act: We told the kids to go find things to do and Cam and I instituted our own private celebration—time to talk, just the two of us, over a shared pot of tea, with the noise of the children in the background.

Making Good Food Choices
Probably because food preparation does not "come naturally" to me, because the office rather than the kitchen is the room

in which I feel most competent and at home, I have always had to *think* about nutrition. And because I have at various times been very short of dollars, I have had to really *think* about value too.

To confirm and correct some of my own hunches about making good food choices, especially when on a stringently limited budget, I met with Dr. Deanna Swinamer, a young doctor who has not only her M.D. but also a B.Sc. in nutrition and a M.Sc. in experimental medicine. She is a registered dietician as well as a family physician. Dr. Swinamer stressed that people do not need to buy special products in order to be healthy — but they do need to learn to think intelligently about food.

We talked about making good choices in the various food groups areas. About *fat,* Dr. Swinamer says, "It's a lot more important just to cut down on fat in general, always choosing lower fat foods, for instance, than to know the difference between polyunsaturated and saturated fats," she says. "In general, the North American diet has too much fat in it — so watch for the lower milk fat (M.F.) or butter fat (B.F.) figures on products like cheese and yogurt. There is no need for fanaticism — small quantities of fat won't hurt you. But just make a general rule of using less fat, choosing lower fat products."

Dr. Swinamer likes to use broth for sautéing vegetables rather than fat, and suggests that it be bought dehydrated in bulk to serve as a base for stir fries or fried rice. What about peanut butter, every mother's best friend? It is inexpensive and can be counted on to be a favorite with most children. "Peanut butter is fine," Dr. Swinamer says. "If I were a mother of young kids, would I buy a big can of generic-brand peanut butter? You bet I would. It's good nutrition, especially if combined with mashed banana. But why not just hold the margarine or butter, so you are not doubling up on the fat content of a sandwich?"

Protein, Dr. Swinamer says, "has taken a beating. But we need protein — and for most people, red meat is needed in the diet. Our bodies do not store protein, so daily intake is necessary. It's especially important for adolescent girls who are unlikely to get adequate iron and protein from other sources," she says. "If people would just buy lean beef and pork and remember that a recommended serving size of three ounces is much smaller than most people realize, they could eat meat without worrying about it."

She recommends using "meat stretchers" — smaller amounts of meat are needed in a casserole dinner than when served alone. Tinned tuna or salmon can be mixed with mayonnaise and yogurt for a nutritious spread on whole wheat bread or bagels. (Actually, I had an elderly woman describe to me the greatest meat stretcher I ever heard of: she called it "Potato and Point.")

> "We were so poor when I was a child on the east coast," she told me, "that we used to have what we called 'potato and point.' We would cook a tiny portion of meat, usually pork, and the fragrance of that meat would fill the whole house with a wonderful smell. And then my mother would suspend that little piece of meat over the table where we could all enjoy its aroma and serve us the usual huge pot of potatoes. With each bite, we would point our forks toward the meat and imagine its flavor, and then eat our potatoes with the taste of salt pork." (Now, that's stretching it!)

There are, of course, vegetable sources of protein that should be added into our diets: Peas and lentils and a whole range of beans provide cheap and excellent protein sources, better known in some other cultures than in traditional North American food patterns. We are beginning to learn from Mexican and other Hispanic people how to use these sources of protein, both as meat-stretchers and as meat-replacers in our diets.

Carbohydrates, Dr. Swinamer suggests, can be provided inexpensively in a whole range of ways. Pasta is wonderful: cheap and available in many different shapes and forms, it provides carbohydrates, some protein, "and it lasts forever," she says. There is an increasing awareness of the importance of carbohydrates. Current American guidelines suggest that these should supply 50–60 percent of the daily caloric intake.

Since weight-loss programs often come down hard on carbohydrates, we need to remember that it is *bread* that is the universal "staff of life."

Fiber can be added not only through whole-grain breads and cereals but also through what Dr. Swinamer describes as "free vegetables" — that is, vegetables which supply minerals, vitamins, and fiber, but almost no calories. In her list of such free vegetables, she includes mushrooms, celery, lettuce, cucumbers, and bean sprouts.

"People should keep these 'free' vegetables in mind when they are thinking of snacks for their children," Dr. Swinamer says. "And popcorn! Just think how inexpensive it is if you pop it yourself — and it fills without adding a whole lot of calories."

Dr. Swinamer believes in "value-added" meals — adding the value to inexpensive food by home cooking rather than eating preprocessed and packaged food. She herself loves to cook homemade soups like beef barley and vegetable and serve them with homemade biscuits. "Homemade food is much cheaper than processed," she says, "and almost all processed or prepackaged food is higher in fat, higher in salt, and lower in nutrition than the food you prepare yourself."

Like many nutritionists, Dr. Swinamer has a healthy scepticism about food fads that add to the cost of basic nutrition. The idea that "organically grown" food is somehow superior she dismisses as a "trendy popular myth." She would concur with the statement, "There is no scientific basis for claiming that organic foods are more nutritious than conventional foods. Food grown by chemical processes do not necessarily differ in taste, appearance, or nutrient content from those that are grown organically."[2] As a food producer, my husband is troubled by the way in which the media can swing public opinion on matters like "organically grown food." All food grows organically; there is no other way for it to grow. The nutrients that are transformed into food by a plant are the same, whether supplied by chemical or animal by-product fertilizer. The use of chemical fertilizers has brought about a consistent, low-priced supply of nutritious food. But today, nutritionally anxious young people may spend much more than is necessary for good food.

I asked Dr. Swinamer about some other "food anxieties" which may affect food habits, especially for nutritionally conscious people. Do we need vitamin supplements? Not usually, she thinks, provided we are eating a varied diet with a daily intake of fruit and vegetables. "But I don't think there is anything wrong with taking a one-a-day supplement," she says. "I wouldn't spend money on anything special, though—just a generic supplement. There is no evidence that we need such supplementation, but many people feel it's better to be on the safe side, and I see no problem with that."

And what about concerns that food from organs like liver are dangerous as sources of cholesterol? Dr. Swinamer thinks that liver is fine—and still an important source of iron. "If you keep your diet low-fat overall, you don't have to be unduly concerned about cholesterol," she says. And she dismisses worries about eggs as a source of cholesterol too. "Eggs are fine as long as the overall diet is low in fat. They are a good, cheap source of protein."

Dr. Swinamer sums up her healthy, informed, and balanced nutritional stance by saying, "Keep the fat down, and eat what you want!"

The 1990 Dietary Guidelines for Americans include the following:
1. Eat a variety of foods.
2. Maintain a healthy weight.
3. Choose a diet low in fat, saturated fat, and cholesterol.
4. Choose a diet with plenty of vegetables, fruits, and grain products.
5. Use sugars only in moderation.
6. Use salt and sodium only in moderation.
7. If you drink alcoholic beverages, do so in moderation.[3]

Shopping Tips

If you start from a position of basic understanding concerning the basic components of a balanced and nutritious diet, you can begin to plan shopping a little better. Especially on a limited budget, shopping is a task that demands real commitment and ability. Here are a few angles I learned in the lean years that might make your grocery cart a little easier to push around.

1. *Shop from a list.* This will help you avoid impulse buying, something which is promoted in every aisle of today's stores. Remember, your grocery store manager takes courses in how to tempt you to buy more than you need. You have to be prepared to outwit the most sophisticated psychological techniques as well as your own appetite if you are to keep your food basket uncluttered. Your shopping list can be made up in the following two ways, both of which I have used:

• *Draw up your list after planning your menus for the week.* This is a great idea for new homemakers, or for old ones who want to get out of food ruts. Planning this way will take you about an hour a week, after you have prepared a card index of menus with recipes to match. By following the basic food rules in setting up your menu cards, you can plan meals that are interesting and varied and nutritional. Then, looking up the recipes, you can list for purchase just those ingredients you will need for one week's meals. This is thrifty, and possibly the best way to teach yourself how to plan a balanced diet for your family.

• *Keep a running list of basic food supplies.* This should be fastened inside a cupboard door or somewhere else handy, with every member of the family jotting down items which need to be replenished as they run low. While I used the method outlined above for the first few years of marriage, this is the method we haved used for years in compiling our shopping lists. That's why my list used to show such items as "Toylet Payper," added by a seven-year-old making her contribution to keeping up basic supplies.

2. *Shop no more than once a week.* This may not be practical if you walk to your store and carry home your groceries, though there are small push-or-pull carts (and I don't mean the

ones that are supposed to be left at the store!) that you can get to bring home two or three bags. But if you drive to do your shopping, then once a week is the best way to shop. It has been my unfailing experience that every time I run into a grocery store for "some little thing" I neglected getting during my main shopping trip, I find myself picking up several other "little things," and food costs begin to escalate.

3. *Leave the children at home if you can.* Small children are precious and interesting, without a doubt. But in the aisles of a grocery store, they are just an added complication. Falling from grocery carts is now one of the most frequent causes of early childhood injury — so there, now you can leave them out of your grocery shopping trips for the sake of their health, instead of just your own.

It seems like a good division of labor for one member of the family to become the food-buying specialist. Whoever takes on that task should probably do the shopping alone if at all possible, without the interrupting assistance of little children. No matter how earnestly you may wish to take children's wishes into account, the time for children to express their food preferences is scarcely at the time you are trying to make price comparisons and keep the grocery cart off another shopper's heels.

By the time children are ten or so, they could be involved in helping with the shopping, and really taught how to shop — but earlier than that, they will add to both the cost and stress of a shopping trip. And when you are shopping on a very limited budget, there is plenty of stress built into family shopping without any additional pressure.

4. *Cut down on the number of canned and "almost ready" foods.* Most things are cheaper the further they are from being table-ready. And, as we have already discussed, the less packaged the food is, the lower its cost and the higher its nutritional value is likely to be. Peeling your own potatoes, soaking and baking your own beans, making your own soups, and buying pastas in bulk, instead of in ready-to-heat forms, are just some of the ways you can trim costs. The less you use your can

opener, the better. And, as a side benefit, the garbage gets easier to handle too.

5. *Skip the party foods aisle.* Tiny crackers, squeezable and disposable cheese packages, and other tidbit foods, many with built-in waste that still makes me wince, are often low in nutrition and high in cost. Even for party times, you might want to consider less expensive alternatives — such as your own hot-from-the-oven baking. Your guests are likely to be delighted with something plain and old-fashioned. I still remember one of the most memorable evening lunches ever served to me. It was served to us by Aunt Violet, an aunt of Cam's whom I met only the one time when, as newlyweds, we found ourselves in her town and dropped in for a visit. Caught with unexpected company, she served us tea accompanied by homemade bread and her own peach jam — all served with simple elegance and, best of all, without apology. Remembering that lunch helped me go on offering hospitality even when I could not afford expensive "fixings."

6. *Take it easy on the drinks.* Carbonated drinks, loaded with fizz and sugar and dye, may be popular with young people, but they do not make good nutritional sense. We found that we could save pop for special occasions — and then, most often, stretch it by adding it to fruit juice rather than serving it by itself. Powdered "fruit" drinks too strike me as an expensive way to buy dyed sugar. I still prefer to buy real fruit juice (usually frozen) and skim milk.

When our budget was at its tightest, we were blessed with having a cow to milk — not too feasible a solution for most of you, I imagine. But before we started milking for our family's needs, I mixed whole milk and reconstituted powdered skim milk in equal portions to reduce the cost of milk for four thirsty children. I found that mix — especially if I remembered to mix it up the night before and chill it well — stretched the milk budget without failing the taste test.

7. *Cut down on your use of paper or disposable plastic.* By making your own wipe-up rags from old clothes (soft T-shirts worn very thin are ideal), you can use, wash, and reuse instead

of buying disposable wipe-up cloths and towels. You can encourage your children to keep their tissues in their pockets for a second or third blow. Of course, this thrifty system often means that the tissues will go through the washing machine too! When it comes to paper products, what makes good economic sense makes good ecological sense, too. Just think, along with the dollars, of the trees your family can save.

8. *Buy less sugar and few presweetened products.* The rise in sugar consumption is a phenomenon of our affluence as a society. "Here is an example of how rising affluence over the years changes our kitchen habits," writes Doris Janzen Longacre. "My grandmother iced cakes only for birthdays. My mother iced most of her cakes, but thinly and only between the layers and on top — not on the sides. Until recently I stirred up an ample bowlful of frosting that covered everything and left plenty of finger-lickin's."[4]

Your family may be able to learn, as ours did, to get along with very much less sugar than we had at one time used. Remembering that natural sugars contained in fresh fruits and vegetables are better for us than processed sugar, we got used to meals without desserts apart from seasonal fruit, and that helped us trim not only our grocery budget but also our weight.

9. *Grow a garden.* Clearly, growing a garden is not an option for every family, though even apartment-dwellers might be able to find ways to grow at least salad vegetables in windowbox or patio gardens. Because we lived on a farm where sometimes it seemed that the only thing we did have was space, we found growing a garden to be a great project for the whole family, with the homegrown vegetables providing a bonus in both nutrition and flavor. The children used to work with me in the garden. On hot days, we would set out a goal — perhaps, "Let's each hoe two rows" or "Let's get the peas picked," with the promise of a cool-down swim and picnic when the job was done. Unlike many of my neighbors, I never did get to be much of a canner or pickler or jam-maker, and I must be quite honest, I am still less than a rapturous gardener. But we did

work together as a family to put away each year all that we would need by way of frozen and root vegetables.

10. *In the midst of the pressure, grow a grateful heart.* It is easy to get focused on finances and forget how wonderfully we are provided for. And again, I suppose it was in the times when we no longer took daily and weekly provision for granted that we learned real gratitude. I can remember the cashier at our local co-op store wincing as she rang up the bill for my weekly shopping — which, by the time our kids were in their teens and we had a couple of hired people working in the summer, looked more like an order for a summer camp. "This is going to hurt," she said. Maybe because I have known times when I couldn't stock up, couldn't buy beyond the immediate needs, I could only protest, "Goodness, no. It doesn't hurt. I'm glad to have a family and hired people to feed and to live in a country where I can feed them."

In this hungry world of ours, where for many there is a daily struggle just to survive, we are the fortunate ones. Even when most pressed, most of us have only the problem of making wise choices.

Food, then, is first a matter of the head, as we study the facts of sound nutrition. And then it is a matter of the heart, as we share food lovingly with our families and with others. Sharing a meal is still the most open method of hospitality, the one which invites the outsider most deeply into the heart of your family life. Finally, food becomes a spiritual matter as we truly worship our Creator and Provider before each meal, not just in a mumbled grace, but in truly felt and clearly expressed gratitude.

Clothing

"If we have food and clothing, we will be content with that," writes Paul to the young pastor, Timothy (1 Tim. 6:8). And, as we meet our own needs and those of our family, we will have to group clothing with food as a "basic need." In *Fig-Leafing through History,* authors Christie Harris and Moira Johnston attack the notion that clothing is basically either for ornamentation or for seduction. Examining the history of costume, they conclude that clothing represents a very basic human need: the need to be covered.[5]

We need to be covered to define the line between our private and our public selves; to insulate our unfurred bodies from heat and cold; and to create a statement about our sense of self and self-worth. From the Genesis account of the Fall of our first parents in the Garden of Eden, we know that there is some link between clothing and our sense of sin, some way in which the transparency of relationships before the Fall is no longer available to us. But beyond that, we simply know that by modesty we transcend shame; that clothing, as it did in the Garden when God supplied Adam and Eve with animal skins to cover and warm them, continues to exemplify God's grace in dealing with us. And our care in dress demonstrates our appreciation for the bodies God has given us. How we look does affect the way we feel about ourselves — and the way in which others respond to us. Especially when we are in times of financial restraint, we need to find ways to celebrate ourselves in attractive clothing without overspending or becoming obsessed with the latest fashions.

Clothing our young people these days poses conundrums. While the things that frugal people have worn for years have become highly stylish, the young people I teach at the university are more likely than the working poor to wear ragged (and unpatched) jeans. There are always subtleties of brand name and styling to remind that these "looped and windowed" clothes are worn as a matter of choice and not of necessity.

In the matter of dress as well as the matter of food, we learned how faithfully God provides. Here — from my clothes closet to yours — are a few of the things we learned about clothing a growing family while having to keep up to date ourselves for lives which included political and professional involvement as well as platform speaking and television appearances — often on a shoestring budget.

1. *Sewing and mending.* In the '90s, torn and unpatched clothes have become trendy among teenagers — but most of us

are still glad to know how to patch and mend creatively. Tightening buttons as soon as a garment is purchased can sometimes save the frustration and expense of replacing a whole set of buttons. Patching worn children's clothes with bright fabric can extend the life of the garment and renew its style.

Even though I would rather write a book than thread a needle, I patched, mended, and sewed clothes for the children until they went to school. In fact, I became quite creative in the ways I mended whole boxes full of hand-me-downs from older cousins to keep the kids in renewed play clothes at little cost. When the sewing machine I had bought before I was married could no longer stand up to mending denim jeans and coveralls, I used one of my first writing checks to replace it. And I helped all my children learn how to use the sewing machine for projects of their own. Despite being among the least gifted seamstresses in the world, I still claim the credit for having taught our daughter Camille, now a doctor preparing to become a surgeon, how to take her first stitches.

For many years, my wardrobe was a handmade gift to me by an older woman in the community who took me into her heart when I arrived as a new bride about the same time her own children were leaving home. With a keen love for fabric and a strong sense of style, Elsie sewed for me (as well as for her daughters and daughter-in-law, all close to me in age and size), providing me with distinctive custom-made clothes I could never have afforded otherwise. She crowned the many years of loving ministry-by-needle by making wedding gowns for both of our daughters, each gown created with loving attention to detail and fitted to perfection by "Aunt Elsie."

For families where both spouses work outside of the home, the time that home-sewing takes would have to be evaluated against other claims. However, a sewing machine in the home means that sewing tasks as small as routine hemming or mending and as large as making new drapes can be done at a much lower cost than if they were custom done. (And, by the way, if you get joy out of sewing, doing these same tasks for others who do not have the time or equipment may be a source of income you can earn right at home.) For many stay-at-homers, sewing provides a double joy — the pleasures of frugality and of creativity. For some, it may also be a source of income or a mode of ministry.

2. *Recycling.* Buying good quality clothes at consignment or other types of resale stores no longer has any stigma attached. In fact, it is considered very smart to know how to find and wear a bargain. An acquaintance of mine who dresses like the model she once was, boasts that she has never yet spent more than fifty dollars on any one item of clothing — yet she always looks like a million. Her tip is that to spend a few dollars on a current fashion magazine (cheaper yet to read them at the public library) may save you several hundred in clothing purchases. Once you know the "look" you want, you can shop frugally at next-to-new stores.

When it comes to dressing children, I suggest you get in the slipstream just behind a family with children a year or two older than yours! Everyone needs to have someplace to send all those still-good clothes that are not worn out. It might as well be your house. I gladly received hand-me-downs, and made a newly arrived box a matter of celebration with the children. We would go through what was passed on to us with curiosity and delight (yes, and quite irreverent try-ons) and then choose what to keep and what to package up and pass on to the Salvation Army.

Pleasure at being able to share clothes was an old one for me. My mother had modeled the "gratitude attitude"; my sisters and I passed our clothes down to each other and later, when we were all much the same size, shared clothes to multiply our wardrobes. So I was stunned and very offended when one day I offered some outgrown clothes of our children's to a young mother. Though she had just been complaining about the high cost of kids' clothes, she drew herself up and replied scornfully, "We're not *that* hard up."

"Well," I said (and not as tranquilly as it looks in print), "I guess we have always been that hard up." I have never thought that recycling good clothes was evidence of anything but good sense, glad sharing, and God's provision.

3. *Shopping and selection.* Shopping at end-of-season sales still strikes me as one of the best ways to buy new clothes at reasonable prices. The winter clothing needed in the northern states and in Canada is expensive, but much less so if you can watch for the late winter clearance sales and outfit your family a year ahead.

As children grow up, they need to have a greater voice in their clothing choices. After all, they are the ones who have to wear those clothes among their schoolmates. Clothing is a powerful element in establishing self-esteem, especially among today's status-conscious young.

I needed to be reminded of that by my own teenagers. I recall driving to town for shopping with them one day. In the backseat, I could hear discussion about what brand was "in" and what was "out." In a voice of maternal authority, I pronounced, "The brand name just doesn't matter."

"Oh," said my son's voice from behind me, "but it does, Mom, it does."

And he was, of course, right. In the culture in which the kids lived, brand names were part of the silent language of the hallways. The only way I could solve the tension between my sense of "value" and theirs was to assign to each of them a clothing allowance and let them make their own choices. If buying one pair of jeans "shot the wad," they would have to wait for other items on their lists. They learned to save for big-ticket items and to make choices, and, as a result, we didn't have so many arguments to deal with.

* * *

"See how the lilies grow," Jesus said (Matt. 6:28). From the field flowers, we can learn not only of God's good provision, but the joy of individuality and variety, the fun of color and texture. Clothing, carefully chosen and tastefully worn, need not be an endless hassle and should not be a source of worry. Rather, as a carefully thought-through and well-planned part of life, clothing becomes a joyful affirmation of our personal dignity and worth, and a source of praise to God, the giver of all good gifts.

Ten Ways to Save Money Now

1. Examine credit card spending. Studies indicate that the convenience of a credit card results in a 30 percent increase in spending.

2. Stay out of shopping malls. The average time spent per visit to a shopping mall is 69 minutes. Only 52 percent of shoppers surveyed spend less than one hour when shopping. A lot of damage can be done in one hour with your credit card.

3. For a good return on investment, pay your credit card debt. The interest charges you save in paying off your credit card debt are much higher than the interest you would receive if you had an investment of equal value at a bank.

4. Begin saving tax dollars. Read the tax credits and deductions listed in the booklet with your income tax return. Retirement fund contributions and charitable donations are two examples of how you can plan for retirement and reduce taxes. Consider making a contribution to your retirement fund and giving the refund to charity.

5. Compare auto insurance rates. Rates can vary substantially from one agency to another, and the quality of coverage may be the same. The benefits from researching rates and coverage can add up real savings!

6. Examine your grocery shopping bill. Begin using coupons and purchasing sale items only. You will watch your food expenditures drop by 15 percent.

7. If you eat lunch in restaurants during the week, limit this to one day per week, and not payday (you will spend too much). You will save nearly $30 per week, and this may total $1,500 in a year!

8. Decide to save a portion of your income each week. Even $5 per week will give you over $250 extra at year end.

9. If you are traveling on the same route as family members or coworkers, consider carpooling. Sharing expenses with only one other person will reduce transportation costs by 50 percent, provide companionship for the ride, and help our environment!

10. Prepare a gift list. Plan your gift ideas, and purchase them in advance when gift items are on sale. Better still, make a gift; it will be special and have far more value to the recipient.

Remember, last-minute shopping always costs more, sometimes up to 40 percent!

— Used by permission from "His Ways & Our Means," January 1994, © Inter-Varsity Christian Fellowship of Canada.

Chapter Eight

Basic Needs III:
Housing and Wheels

Wheels

Like many families, we found the problem of providing adequate housing for our family to be a difficult one. While food and clothing are the bare minimum basics when it comes to needs, nobody disputes that housing is an essential too. Bewildered by ever-rising costs of home construction and struggling with straightening out real housing values — space for a family, sufficient individual privacy, warmth for our long, cold winters — from those confusing transferred values — status, snobbery, "pride of life," we spent several winters in cramped rented accommodations as we thought and prayed and waited.

Part of the North American way of life until the last two or three decades has been not only a place to call home but a place to call your own. Even a Willy Loman, the loser salesman in Arthur Miller's *Death of a Salesman,* is able to buy a little house and put himself into fixing it up. Today, the high costs of land and housing have pushed this possibility of home ownership well out of the reach of many people, or pushed young married people into the necessity of earning two incomes in order to meet heavy payments on long-term mortgages.

We have to face the fact that the inaccessibility of affordable family dwellings reflects not only the high cost of housing, but also the high cost of furnishings. Television has piped the big dream into our living rooms for so many hours that we really begin to think of "home" in terms of the sets for television dramas. We have to struggle to remember that the shows have been brought to us, hour after hour, by the producers of goods who want us to want and consume things and who encourage us to develop extravagant tastes so that we will buy, buy, and go on buying.

I learned quite a bit by living in the tiny house the Lord provided for us as a "shelter in the time of storm." Our family of six lived in about 800 square feet of space (not counting a damp basement, where there was space for my washer and drier). There were three small bedrooms, two of them upstairs under the eaves, with the bats twittering in the attic on the other side of the thin walls and occasionally escaping into the house. We turned the downstairs bedroom into an office and finally made the living room double as a bedroom by means of a convertible sofa. We felt cramped, all right. If one of the kids brought a balloon home from a party, I felt as though someone was going to have to leave to make room for it. And then there was the time when all the kids and Cam got mumps together!

Certainly, compared with the houses people were building around us, our housing was inadequate, and yet we had to stop once in awhile to remember that a generation earlier, a family of four grew to adulthood in this very house. A family of six plus a hired girl. What had changed? Were children bigger than they had been a generation ago? Or were our housing concepts just bigger?

We had to admit, as we thought about it, that our need for large houses reflects our growing accumulation of things far more than a real need for more space for people. It is particularly ironic that as houses get bigger, families get smaller. Let's face it, more and more people are finding they just cannot afford both a big house and a big family. Because we had to do a lot of thinking about housing, we became aware of a range of resourceful solutions to the problem of adequate housing. Perhaps one of these will be the solution for you, as it was for us.

1. *Work to save a down payment and then buy a modest house.*

You can take a twenty-five or thirty-year mortgage, recognizing that housing always costs (usually about 24 percent of disposable income), but that real estate has customarily responded to inflation. This means that your home, if well maintained, is likely to increase in value over the years. Home ownership has been one of the "little person's" surest investments, supplying a basic need for the family as the property value increases.

2. *Buy an older, run-down house and have the joy of restoring it to life.* This, of course, depends on your having the skills for renovating, since that will represent the "sweat equity" you put into your house and recover when you sell it. Even more, it will depend upon the whole family having the patience to live in the mess of ongoing construction—something not everyone can stand. But if you have the skills and temperament for living in a half-finished project, it may work for you. We know a successful building contractor who started his business in just this way, moving into a run-down house, upgrading it and then reselling it. Then he moved into another and did the same, until he had the capital—and the experience—he needed for launching his own custom building business. Nor does this method of home ownership provide only inexpensive housing for the family. It also provides ongoing renewal for urban areas which might otherwise downgrade into slums. On the negative side, of course, are the social problems of "gentrification," by which renewed and renovated older homes in centrally located urban neighborhoods become trendy homes for the well-to-do young and are pushed up in price out of the reach of the poor. If you are considering this buy-up-grade-sell approach to gradually improving your housing, you might also have to consider whether you are comfortable with moving your family into the kind of neighborhood in which run-down houses tend to be found. What kind of schools are there? How safe are the streets? After weighing the pros and cons, you may decide that this is the right choice for you. And if you do, think about looking for a church just around the corner, and becoming part of the ministry in the area in which

you are living. That way you can become part of building something more permanent even than your home.

3. *Buy a house with an apartment in the basement or elsewhere.* Be sure before doing this to check zoning regulations to ascertain that you can legally rent it out. Or move into a duplex and rent the other half. You will have to give up some of your privacy and some of the elegance of a place all to yourself, but the extra revenue could well cover your mortgage payments, thus making it possible for you to purchase your own real estate.

4. *Consider the possibility of building your own place.* This is something which more and more young people are doing now. You can buy precut houses, or save even more by buying the dimensional lumber and building a home yourself. Be realistic in estimating your savings, remembering that you will still have to hire subcontractors to do the work in which you are not skilled. And don't forget that it will take time and grit to see a project like this through to completion. Some additional precautions are: Be sure to check carefully the housing regulations covering the area where you intend to build; remember that you will need help and perhaps a labor exchange with one or more friends. Outside of city limits (or even within some), you may be able to build a basement and finish enough to live in it, and then build your house over your head. Habitat for Humanity, the home-building program that ex-President Jimmy Carter has made so visible, may provide a way for you to build—or help someone else to build—a place to call home. (Habitat for Humanity International, Inc., 121 Habitat Street, Americus, GA 31709-3498.)

5. *Build, or have built, a small house with a design and on a lot which are suitable to future expansion.* This may be a way to save interest if you can pay for the first part of the house before going on with the next phase. Friends of ours have built a spacious family home in this way. Starting with a cozy two-bedroom bungalow when they were first married, they have expanded the house in two phases as the needs of their family have grown, imaginatively adapting a simple basic plan to meet

their family's special tastes and requirements.

6. *If you already own a home, consider all the possibilities for developing your present property.* A developed basement or attic or a built-on addition may be enough to make your house meet your family's needs, probably at far less expense than buying a new home at today's prices. When Barb and Jim found that their three-bedroom bungalow, bought ten years ago, was beginning to feel a bit snug, they began to look at new housing. When they calculated the cost of a move to a larger house, they found that they could much more economically develop the one they already had. A basement development project doubled the amount of their living space at far less cost than the same number of square feet would cost at today's prices. My cousin Rodger Woods is an architect who has found a way to make a small old brick house big enough for his family through the ingenious use of the existing space and the planning (and hand-building) of several additions: first, kitchen and dining areas, later, an expanded upstairs. There are many exciting ways to make your present home "do," providing that you own it and can get city council approval for proposed renovations.

7. *A more radical idea, but one that is increasingly interesting to young families, is to solve your housing problems away from a major city.* Consider moving out to the country and buying an old farmhouse to rebuild, or building your own new home on an acreage or in a small town. But don't let the lure of the land draw you into an ill-advised move. Consider carefully the job opportunities suitable to your skills within a reasonable driving radius. A necessity for this way of life is dependable vehicles, probably two, since a person left stranded ten miles from anywhere is sure to feel insecure. So include the cost of extra transportation in your figuring. And be sure you get someone experienced in home building to assess the soundness and give you an estimate of the cost of fixing up that romantic old house you fall in love with before you start in on something quite unrealistic.

The advantages of this approach to housing are becoming

apparent to more and more young people who like the idea of
raising their children away from the "thickening centre."[1] We
are seeing farmhouses that have stood empty for years being
bought and lived in. Five-acre plots can still be purchased in
more remote rural areas for a fraction of the cost of an average
city lot. I am not talking about moving to the plush acreage
suburbs of a large city which are customarily inhabited by
doctors, lawyers, and chiropractors. Rather, I am referring to
getting far out into the country, a hundred miles or more from
major cities. Only then is there any real economy in this concept. And I am *not* talking about "going farming" as a way to
solve the housing dilemma. Farming is a big business and a
risky one. Trying to live off the land is to reduce living to a
subsistence, virtually no-cash level, which is very difficult for
inexperienced or even experienced people. What I am talking
about is practicing your trade or profession in a small town or
city within a reasonable driving radius (probably 50 miles or
so) and enjoying the quiet of country or small-town living. You
can live for less in the country because you can grow your own
garden, keep a cow, and raise chickens — and children — on a
place of your own. You need fewer "good" clothes, but transportation is expensive and continuous. Utilities characteristi-
cally cost a great deal more than in the city, but you have to
develop and maintain your own water and sewage system outside of a town or city. So everything does not come up roses.
However, it is an option worth considering — carefully.

8. *A low-cost answer to housing is mobile or prefab homes.*
Mobile homes sometimes do not have the status, the eye appeal, or the prestige of other homes. And, unfortunately, many
of the subdivisions in urban areas for mobile homes are unattractive and ridiculously crowded. However, more and more
municipalities are beginning to zone proper-sized lots for mobile homes, recognizing that mobile homes do not represent
transience as much as lower-cost housing, deserving of dignity
as a practical solution to the pressing problem of housing for
young families. One thing that must be weighed against the
initial price advantage is that mobile homes have customarily

depreciated in value, while properly maintained fixed dwellings customarily appreciate. Quality of insulation and wiring needs to be carefully checked, since the fire hazard of mobile homes, with the large amount of flammable glue used in their construction, must be taken into consideration.

9. *Obviously, apartment or semidetached dwellings will increasingly be the normal housing for most newly married urban couples and for many families as well.* Since there is a wide range of differences as well as costs in today's apartments and condominiums, this may be the kind of housing which you prefer, or it may be what you can afford. Whatever the case, your apartment home can be "a light shining in a dark place" (2 Peter 1:19), your family a Christian witness in the apartment or condominium complex in which you live. The very proximity to other people, which often affords many problems, can also offer limitless opportunities to befriend, to witness, to show the love and life of Christ. Many choose this type of housing, knowing that home ownership involves a multitude of other concerns and costs: lawns to be mowed, storm windows put up and taken down again, and an endless round of maintenance. When I have watched apartment dwellers place their key cards in the automatic door opener of their underground garage, I have mused about the simple life. All the folklore to the contrary, the simple life may well be apartment living.

Which of these was our solution?

Well, we had property in the country, so it made sense to build there. A year or two after our business failed, we had our financial affairs in order again and approached the credit manager of our credit union. Would it be possible for us to get a mortgage for a very modest home? We had priced out mobile homes and had some figures for him. We had sat there so often, it seemed: Going over figures, explaining our situation and our plan for repayment of debt, making payments. We waited anxiously while he looked at our proposal and then across his desk at us. In my mind I rehearsed what I thought we would hear: It would, I thought, sound something like, "We certainly understand your need for a home, but your present circumstances would not allow for any further extension of credit. . . ." Or, perhaps, "Why don't you come back and see us in a year or two?"

Instead, the credit manager stubbed out his cigarette and cleared his throat and said, "You folks don't really want a mobile home, do you? Why don't you go get some prices on a house and bring them in to me."

We did. With his encouragement, we shopped for a modest plan that we could modify to meet our needs, determined not to borrow one more dollar than we needed to supply our family with a comfortable home. And then we had the house built. By building into a hill so that the front of the basement was ground level and full of light, and by developing both upper and lower levels fully, we had ample space under a small roof, doubling our 1,250 square feet in living space. What a joy to have a generous entryway with a wash-up bathroom at the back door, a laundry room, an office, small but adequate bedrooms for each of the children, a separate playroom, and a "great room," a large open living-dining-kitchen area. We even have a tiny *en suite* bathroom off our compact "master bedroom." This was not the glossy show-home of the "country homes" magazines, but a comfortable, affordable home suited to our needs as a family. We had lots of windows to let in light from all directions, lots of walls to gradually fill in with bookshelves, and a special wall in the open living-dining-kitchen area where, years later, we would install a beautiful cast iron wood-burning stove on a raised hearth, set against a blue-gray stone facing.

When we moved into our new home, our children were in elementary school; through the rest of their growing-up years, the home fit our family like a glove — sometimes a very snug glove. True enough, one of the kids had to give up a bedroom when company came; for several years a spare cot in the laundry room was where one of them slept during the summers we had live-in hired help for our farm. Later, we were able to move a separate small summer house onto our farmstead, for "extras."

"Today's home buyer wants space that can be adjusted to meet new needs over time. . . . Secondary bedrooms [are] proportionally bigger. And the addition of private bathrooms makes them better suited for use down the road by adult children or older parents who return to the home,"[2] declared a recent newspaper article.

Well in advance of such housing trends being announced, we built our fully finished ground-level basement floor so that it could serve as a separate suite of rooms, thinking that perhaps one day one of our parents might need a sunny sitting room, bedroom, and bathroom.

Our children grew up and we moved on, but the house again shelters a young family—now it is our son's family that shelters there, and we have down-sized to a snug, light-filled city apartment, just big enough for the two of us.

Whatever the solution to meeting the housing needs of your family, the real joys of any home are not in the size or shape of the physical plant, but in the spirit of love and contentment that prevails within the walls. As you learn contentment in the situation in which you find yourself, you can trust God to guide you in making the necessary adjustments to make housing adequate for your needs.

Wheels

The ever-present cost pressure of owning and then of operating a family vehicle or two involves major decision-making. When friends of ours decided they had to supplement their family station wagon with a second car, they found an old Ford with a lot of its gray paint chipped off. It was a kind of sad-looking car that their teen sons immediately dubbed "Dog Face." One of the boys' pals looked at the car and hooted, "What's that thing supposed to be?"

"That," said my friend, with the immense dignity she saves for such moments, "is a one-payment car."

They had decided on one of the three options that seem to make good economic sense when it comes to providing dependable transportation at a reasonable cost. Here are the low-cost options as I see them. One may be right for you.

1. *Buy a low-cost used car and drive it until it begins to need major repairs.* When a car begins to burn oil, major motor problems are probably just around the corner. If you suspect problems with either the engine or the transmission, you should probably take the car to a nondealer mechanic and ask for an assessment. Before authorizing any work, you can then decide if the cost of fixing the car is more than the car is worth to you and if so, sell it and start again.

While you can compromise on cosmetics (a car does not have to be pretty), you will want to be uncompromising on safety: tires, brakes, and steering. And for safety's sake, you need to do your trouble-shooting before the car lets you down. Nonetheless, if you need to drive an old car, you might want to consider membership in a motorist association that provides emergency help and towing if necessary. Your car insurance, however, likely will reimburse you for towing.

2. *Buy a premium used car.* This is different from buying a "junker" and driving it until it drops. Buying a premium used car means buying a car of which you know the history, or one which is in excellent condition, and maintaining it for all the extra miles that are in it after its initial depreciation has brought the price down.

After we had watched neighbors buy the two- or three-year-old cars we had traded for newer models, and drive them for another five or six years, we began to take this thrifty route too. Cam tells me that in shopping for a used car, he looks for any indication (beyond the mileage on the odometer) that tells how much, and how hard, the car has been driven. "I look for wear on the brake pedal," he says, since that is one indicator of use that cannot be easily touched up. "And look for any indications of touch-up activity: little spray-over jobs covering rust spots, for instance. I take a close look at the upholstery to see if there are little nicks or tears that, despite a cleanup, would be signs of hard or careless use. And if the car were full of the smell of pine trees, I'd try to figure out what the pine trees were trying to cover.

"I'd avoid any car that looks like it has seen country roads — little gravel chips in the paint, or bent parts underneath. And I'd also avoid anything that had what the kids call 'wide skins' or tires with bold white lettering — which would suggest it has been driven by a teenager.

"I would, of course, pull the dipstick. Usually that's all looked after in preparing a car for sale, of course, but just in case — I'd take a look at the oil. If it were at all dirty, I wouldn't buy. And when I took the car for a test drive, I would check it for overall tightness — in the steering, the drive train, the body.

"If I can get a chance to meet the previous owner, all the better," Cam stresses. "I can study the kind of person who owned the car before — the house and yard, the clothing and attitude. I'm looking for any indication of owner attitude toward the vehicle I am considering buying — and the more persnickety and fussy that person appears to be, the better for me. Of course, I'll ask the reasons for selling the car — and evaluate what the owner tells me."

Sometimes Cam has bought cars directly from their previous owners; sometimes he has bought through a dealer. When we're ready to replace our current car, he lets a salesperson or two know what he is looking for — placing a tentative order and hoping to hear of a good quality car that has come in on trade. And Cam takes a look at a current *Consumer Guide* rating. "A low-mileage lemon may look like a good deal but cost you a lot in the long run," he points out. "I'm more interested in a highly rated car, even if it has been driven a bit longer."

What about the car you are driving right now? "Sell it privately or give it to one of your kids or the mechanic down the street — you'll probably do just as well as trying to trade it in on another used car," Cam says. He points out that the car price jumps approximately 15 percent the minute that a trade-in is involved. Cam suggests that if you really want to unload your current car in the deal, begin the discussion on a no-trade basis so that a price can be established. Then you can ask what the price would look like if you offered your trade-in, and you'll know exactly the difference, exactly what your old used car is deemed to be worth.

The trend in North America toward people keeping their cars longer works against the "premium used car" route to affordable transportation, since it means fewer next-to-new cars on the market and at higher prices than a few years ago. It is still worth taking a look. We have been able to enjoy the comfort and low-cost miles of excellent cars which, had we bought them new, would have cost us a lot more.

3. *Buy a new car and drive it until it reaches the end of its tether.* Perhaps that will be eight or ten years, depending on the number of miles you drive per year. This plan requires that you maintain the car carefully so that it lasts and lasts and lasts. The high depreciation of the first year or two are spread out over as many as ten years, and thus a car bought new can be quite economical.

Of course, there are still many people who can afford to buy new cars every year or two, but others either cannot afford this style or are wondering if there are not more useful ways of spending their money. More and more, people are availing themselves of short courses in mechanical know-how, borrowing or renting garage space, and doing minor and even major repairs on their own vehicles.

A major factor in any new- or used-car decision is gas-mileage economy. For the sake of both economy and the environment, many of us are looking for ways to find our groceries — and probably our church fellowship — within walking distance of our homes, instead of trekking across our cities in endlessly crisscrossing patterns. Who knows? The cost of fuel may even have the effect of keeping some families home together in the evenings, giving them a chance to get to know each other again. Many of us are learning to leave the car in the garage whenever we can, to keep lists so that we make a minimum number of trips to stores, and to walk or bike instead of driving. These "new" concepts of how to get around represent not only savings in expense but also improvement in general physical condition. Walking, jogging, and biking can give us the warm, happy, and slightly choking sensation that we are merely using up pollution instead of creating it.

*   *   *

A place to call home, a means by which to get away from and back to it again, plus our food and clothing constitute basic physical needs. For these we can, in faith, claim God's supply, while at the same time learning to be judicious in our choices.

Chapter Nine

The Other Needs

The young pastor's wife came home from the seminar, crushed and bewildered. "I guess I just don't have enough faith," she said.

"Enough faith for what?" I wondered aloud.

"Well," she explained, "the speaker was telling us how to budget our time and money. But she was so breezy about economic matters. She told us, 'I just believe God wants to give you all good things. Why, He just loves to give you the desires of your heart. Right now, I'm asking the Lord for a South Pacific cruise. And, you know, it's beginning to look as though one is shaping up for us.' " My friend came away from the seminar sick at heart. "A lot of us just don't live at that level. Is it lack of faith? The desire of my heart is to feed and clothe the kids on my husband's salary, never mind the South Pacific cruise!"

The young wife was quite right; most of us do not live at a level where we have the liberty to think of doing some of the things which seem to come so naturally to others. For such a high standard of living to be held out as a norm, achievable by any who dare to exercise faith, is a travesty of Christian values.

A.W. Tozer writes scathingly, "So many professing Christians just want to get things from God. Anyone can write a book now that will sell—just give it a title like *Seventeen Ways to Get Things from God!* . . . Many people seem to be interested in knowing God for what they can get out of Him."[1] In another article, entitled "That Utilitarian Christ," Tozer warns against viewing the Lord Jesus Christ as "a kind of Aladdin's lamp to do minor miracles in behalf of anyone who summons Him," and goes on to say:

> The whole purpose of God in redemption is to make us holy and to restore us to the image of God. . . . He disengages us from earthly ambitions and draws us away from the cheap and unworthy prizes that worldly men set their hearts upon.[2]

From the Reformation acceptance of the intrinsic worth of secular vocations, and the necessity for hard work within those callings, we have moved so far toward complete secularization of our lives that we need to carefully examine everything we read or hear to see if it sounds at all like the lowly Jesus, who had no place to call home, no coin with which to pay His taxes, no wealth except that of the Spirit. And before we lightly quote verses of Scripture as magic passkeys to material blessings, we need to ask seriously about God's purposes in our lives. We must always be aware and afraid of treating God as some kind of heavenly vending machine which will spew out endless material things for our enjoyment simply because we have "faith" and live uprightly.

"God is Spirit: and His worshipers must worship in spirit and in truth" (John 4:24). He is concerned about our material needs insofar as they constitute real needs; Jesus taught us that in the Sermon on the Mount. If, in His bounty, God should give us a measure of prosperity over and above our needs, that is a gift of His disposing, not of our demanding. And it is given to us in trust.

A few years ago, some friends of ours listened to a sermon on faith. The speaker told the story of two women, a mother and a daughter, who were in need of winter coats. The mother prayed (as a member of an older generation might), "Dear Lord, I need a winter coat. Just anything, as long as it is warm, will do." The daughter (a true member of the modern society) prayed, "I need a winter coat too, Lord. But, please, I would like it to be brand-new, size twelve, and green." Each woman got exactly what she had asked for, the preacher said. The gist of the sermon seemed to be: Ask for lots — the very best — and you will get it. Our friends took the sermon very seriously. They understood its message and acted on it. About to build a new house, they scrapped modest, budget-fitting plans they had been thinking about and built a much larger home that brought them to the brink of insolvency.

As economic pressures on the average family increase in the days ahead, we need to speak out against any kind of teaching which suggests that God exists to make us rich, that His special joy is in doling out things. Nothing could be farther from the spirit of the New Testament. There, the dangers of riches are solemnly warned against (for example, 1 Tim. 6:10). There, the norm is "be content with what you have" (Heb. 13:5). There, earthly goods are something to be held in trust; a person's earnings are to enable him to care for his own family and to share with others.

I am sure that many of God's children have known times when God has been pleased to give them the sudden surprise of some delightful material gift. But for the one who is intent on knowing God, that thing, however wonderful it may be, is nothing compared with the hand that gives it, the hand of the great unchangeable giver of all good gifts.

If we study carefully what Jesus said, we will understand that we have no need to be anxious about the supply of our basic needs. They are our right as sons and daughters, heirs in the family of God and will be supplied. But He gives no warrant anywhere for whining and pleading with God for more than our needs, and Paul in his emphasis on self-control echoes his Lord. We can make our requests known. That is our privilege. But to demand, to claim promises out of context, and to expect that righteous behavior should have some earthly tangible reward is pathetically to miss the point.

Charles H. Spurgeon, in commenting on the verse, "You

may ask Me for anything in My name, and I will do it" (John 14:14), makes this thought-provoking observation:

> I may not ask for anything to which I cannot put Christ's hand and seal. I dare not use my Lord's name to a selfish or willful petition. I may only use my Lord's name to a prayer which He would Himself pray if He were in my case. It is a high privilege to be authorized to ask in the name of Jesus as if Jesus Himself asked; but our love to Him will never allow us to set that name where He would not have set it.[3]

I remember one long-ago spring when I had to wait for what seemed an insufferably long time for my paycheck for a part-time job I had taken. I had gone to the university during the winter and had that familiar flat-broke feeling many students have after eight months of steady withdrawals and no deposits. Besides that, I had seen a suit—a beautiful pink suit—in a downtown store. It was lovely and well within the buying power of that check, if and when it would come. Every time I was downtown, I looked to see if the suit was still there. And every time the postman arrived, I looked for that check. Days passed. Still no check. One day, fighting the disappointment of yet another day without the paycheck, I was washing dishes in our basement apartment and arguing with the Lord about it all. "But," I complained, "I've earned that check. Couldn't you just remind someone to mail it to me?" And then a Scripture came so forcibly into my mind that I set down the glass I was washing and listened to it. "When you ask, you do not receive because you ask . . . so that you may spend what you get on your pleasures" (James 4:3).

There were tears in my eyes, but I responded, "OK, Lord. It's not a need. It's just a want." When at the last that check did arrive, I no longer "needed" the pink suit at all.

Over a good many years, even as a very slow learner, I have come to see that far more wonderful than God's giving us every whim we place before Him is the complete—if sometimes painful—job He can do of taking a want out of my heart and then filling the hole it leaves with joy and contentment.

Of course, over and above the basic needs, there are legitimate and recognized needs of the human spirit, mind, and body. With some creative use of available resources, many of these needs too can be met within limited budgets. And life can be full of "extras" without big price tags attached.

1. *The need for spiritual and intellectual stimulation and growth.* I remember listening to my hairdresser, Richard, chattering as he jerked my head and snipped my hair. "There are some people I know, like, they seem to need to go to every training session on the continent. We had a girl, like, in one of our shops, like, who spent every holiday and all of her money traveling from one hairdressing course to another. And, like, I don't think it has too much to do with learning. Just seems that some people, like, just need to go to all those deals to get sort of pepped up—to believe in themselves. But me, I'd just as soon spend my holidays, like, relaxing. I can learn all I need from the trade magazines. Like, guys who run those short courses have gotten very, very rich because of people who just need that kind of inspiration."

I listened with interest because what Richard was saying can be applied to the endless conferences and seminars that many Christians spend their time and money and holidays attending. There is no doubt that we all need fellowship. We all need encouragement. And we all need inspiration from time to time. I have spoken at lots of conferences (without, by the way, getting rich at it) and have letters on file to remind me that these times of getting together for instruction in the Word of God and for mutual encouragement do change lives.

If we have the money to travel for conferences and seminars, then it is a good way to promote personal growth. But if such programs are beyond the reach of our budgets, we need not despair. I have found that God is just as accessible from the square of linoleum that is my kitchen floor as He is from the loftiest mountaintop conference. In fact, when the children were all preschoolers at once, I found the only "retreat center" I could get to was the bathroom.

In the years when we were starting our farming business and our family, many of our just slightly younger friends were knapsacking across Europe, spending some time at L'Abri. Others of our more-established friends were going half-way around the world to attend conferences. I learned, in those years, to answer the question, "Where could I go?" in the words of the spiritual song: "Just to the Lord." Shut in with my family in a tiny farmhouse in Alberta, I found ways to go on growing.

I pored over catalogs of advanced learning programs and seminars in distant and exotic places, and then I settled down to read what the greatest writers have said and thought. I learned to grow mentally and spiritually right in my home. I made reading lists from course outlines and book reviews, and read systematically in whole periods of English literature. I read and reread the Bible often, searching the whole of the Bible for understanding a particular topic. So I was able to go on growing at minimal dollar cost.

I yearned for the day when I would be able to engage in more formal study — and rejoiced when that opportunity did come. But in the meanwhile, I did not sigh and resign myself to stagnation while such opportunities were out of reach, both geographically and financially.

The "need to know" can be satisfied, if you have the means, by formal study or by travel. Lacking those means, it can still be satisfied — or better, whetted — by making use of library facilities. Travel to distant places may be beyond the family budget, but good books, maps, and a globe can help you visit faraway places at little or no expense from the warmth of your own home. Cultivating correspondence with various friends across the world will bring exotic foreign stamps to your mailbox while enlarging the worldview of your whole family. Entertaining in your home will bring the world into your living room.

We recall one evening when, in the little kitchen of our farm home, missionaries from Ethiopia met an agricultural exchange trainee from England. Our guests from Africa began to talk with our boarder from England, and within five minutes they discovered that they had a mutual acquaintance: a young woman who was a daughter of the missionaries' coworkers was in nurses' training with the fiancée of our exchange trainee. For a few exciting moments we felt like we were at the crossroads of the world!

Maintaining our *oneness* with the members of the body of Christ brings news from around the world into our home in the form of letters and mission magazines. We reach back out to that world in giving, in prayer, and in letters. Over the years, through Christian fellowship and other connections, we have established a network of personal friends so that now we have friends in almost every free country on the globe. When and if we should be enabled to travel, there will be friends to greet us wherever we go. That's one of the great pleasures of functioning as part of "the family of God." Meanwhile, with young children, we found that the happiest vacations were spent close to home. Frequent short jaunts to the lake twenty miles from our home, sometimes expanded into overnight camping, were as much fun for our children when they were small as the longer trips we attempted.

Our kids still recall the minor epic journey we made, on a sudden impulse, one Saturday afternoon. We went to a town "down the line" from where we lived—about an hour's drive— and did all the things that people do on holidays: Took a room in a motel, ate Chinese food at a restaurant, and went out to see a Disney double feature. (Yes, they even remember what they saw: *The Legend of Lobo* and *Dumbo*. They cried in both of them.) It was a case of making a lot of memories by spending only a little money. For some reason, we all still remember the magic of that weekend. To our now-grown kids, it is as memorable as most of the longer holidays we took with them as they grew older.

2. *The need for aesthetic pleasure.* There is a very real need of the human mind and spirit to perceive and to create things of aesthetic beauty. The God who "hath made everything

beautiful in His time" (Ecc. 3:11) is the one who, in making us in His image, has planted within us the desire for beauty. It is no pagan wish. Neither is it one which requires wealth to satisfy. Aesthetic appreciation can be developed even if your budget precludes you from concerts and performances of the fine arts. Television brings some fine performances into your home, at little cost. You can enjoy the best of good music on your tape or CD player, purchasing an endless number of listenings for about the price of a good seat in a concert hall. Museums and art galleries are customarily free to visit. And, again, there are books.

But, of course, aesthetic appreciation should not just be reserved for formal expressions. A friend, home on furlough from an appointment in North Africa, strolled with me down our lovely lane. "After the endless brown of dried-out northern Africa, the green is so beautiful," she commented. She noted the shades of green against the blue, late afternoon sky. "You know, I have really come to appreciate the *ministry of nature*." Learning to see, to really see, the beauty of the world around us requires nothing more than the use of the senses with which we come equipped. And whether we look at the patch of sky that is ours from a city window or at a sweeping vista on a country road, we can feed our hearts on beauty until praise is born.

The desire to create things of beauty has been exploited in a booming business in craft kits and do-it-yourself (almost) outfits. Crafts and hobbies are an enrichment of life, but some of them may be out of reach when the budget is tight. Remember, though, that the essence of crafts is "creativity." Thus, the more creative you are in seeing the resources available to you, the more satisfying you will find them. You could try hobby-swapping with friends. When the excitement of their rock tumbler has passed, your family may have exhausted the possibilities of candle-making equipment. So arrange an exchange. Again, the library is your pass to free and inexpensive crafts. Books abound to get you and your family started in developing an artistic or creative bent. If you cannot afford to oil paint, you can surely sketch with pencil or charcoal. And poetry has been written on all sorts of surfaces; you could even use the backs of envelopes for that, as Emily Dickenson did.

Creative expression in music requires some sort of instrument (the least expensive, of course, is the voice), some training, and a great deal of persistent practice. In the mid-'70s we visited in a country home that was still without running water or electric power. But an old upright Bell piano sat against one living room wall, with a propane lamp nearby and sheaves of music piled around. The woman, over eighty and bent with age, sat down and played. Her husband sang in a mellow — if somewhat quavery — tenor voice. He no longer plays his violin, he said, "But that grandson of mine, he can get a great tune out of that fiddle." Poor? Enriched by an afternoon of home-grown music, I thought not. Our little home was loud with music since the children all took piano lessons. In the days before our house was built, we were blessed with such a lack of space that the piano and television were in the same room. By the time three children had practiced after school, there was little time for television viewing. Cam and I would sit in the kitchen while in the living room Cammie picked out a tune on her guitar and on the porch Geoff blasted away on a second-hand trumpet. We wanted music to be part of the intangible riches our children would come to value, and having bought a secondhand piano as one of our earliest household purchases, gave music lessons priority over other "wants" even in our most stringent budgets. Three out of four of our children express appreciation for that — either enjoying musical performances or playing instruments themselves. A fourth still feels it was a waste of money and an encroachment on his life. Well, three out of four is not bad!

3. *The need to feel secure.* This is another need which is hard for people on tight budgets to meet. Security. Peace of mind. And these days, these are not easy to come by. Even when we put away payments in government pension plans, we find ourselves wondering if there is going to be money to meet com-

mitments as the demographic bulge called "The Baby Boom" reaches retirement age. Nonetheless, we have to take some systematic steps toward creating—if not security itself, then at least a sense of security.

Basic steps you can take toward satisfying the need to feel secure include a planned savings program for retirement, insurance to cover immediate needs should one or the other spouse die, and legally drawn wills. We were surprised at a fellowship supper with six other couples to find that three of those couples had not drawn up wills. Even if you feel you have few assets to will, you do need to draw a will with the aid of an attorney—if only to name custodians for your children and beneficiaries for any benefits which may accrue. And you will need to update your will from time to time, as your estate or family grows or as your children grow up and leave home. You may want to go a step further and have an attorney draw up a revocable living trust that includes much more than a simple will and doesn't have to go through probate court proceedings that are costly and delay the execution of your wishes.

4. *The need for leisure and relaxation.* "Any valid inventory of human needs must include the therapy of leisure." So reads an advertisement of a large corporation, with the added note, "Our leisure living communities, pleasure cruises, travel trailers, and motor homes are making life more enjoyable for many people." Ironically enough, the picture accompanying the ad shows a family out biking. Certainly recreation is a need, but it has been made expensive by our high tastes. It is time to remind ourselves that we can enjoy a lake without a boat. We can enjoy a boat without a motor. In some areas, we can ski without driving to the mountains. We can enjoy the winter out-of-doors without a snowmobile. And we can even go camping without a trailer or a motor home. Honest. We have done these things. And so have many others like us.

One summer we took a short camping trip with our family, our total gear being a nine-by-twelve-foot tent, a Coleman cookstove, and sleeping bags. At a lakeside campground, we found a quiet nook in which to pitch our tent, and then strolled down to the pleasant, shallow lake for an evening swim.

As we walked back, we found that we were going to have an opportunity to observe a contrasting camp style at very close range. Squeezed into the site next to ours was an enormous motor home. Our first greeting from the new arrivals was a marshmallow, underdone or overdone, tossed onto the road. We just managed to miss squishing it between our bare toes before composing our faces for a neighborly "Hello." We found the new neighbors friendly. Very. Perhaps their children had never been in something so quaint as a tent before, because they explored it thoroughly. *It's always fun to see how the natives live,* I thought to myself.

The marshmallow roast was still going on. "Want a marshmallow, little kid?" their children asked one of ours. Our children had never seen such big, puffy marshmallows. Ours were the smaller, less expensive variety. When our children offered to bring their own marshmallows and toast them at the fire, the others just laughed. "What do we need your marshmallows for, kid? We've got lots." The parents sat and chatted at the picnic table while Cam and I tried to do a bit of camp cooking. Were we going to fry our steaks in that little cooking pot? "Martha, go get our big skillet for these people." Was it getting a bit too dark for me to read? "Martha, get that big flashlight."

The party broke up early. "We've got to get an early start," the father explained. "We're going to do the mountains tomorrow." I thought about that as I crawled into our little tent. Do the mountains tomorrow! The Rockies? Should make a fairly full day! Except for the insistent barking of our neighbors' huge German shepherd, the quiet night beside the lake was undisturbed. Then, soon after six in the morning, the sound of a mighty motor filled the somnolent campground. The great engine fired, roared, then died. Again. And again. Inside our tent, the smell of raw gas was choking, and I was bidding a tearless "Adieu" each time the motor fired hopefully. Finally, the motor took hold, and after several long, throaty revs, our neighbors roared off. They were having a wonderful camping trip, they had told us.

More and more young families are seeking leisure and recreation in activities which are quiet, use muscles instead of motors, and — where possible — can be done "far from the maddening crowd." The beauty of it all is that many of these activities can be enjoyed at minimum cost. There never has been a price put on a sunset. Or moonrise. Or the quiet glow of a dying campfire beside a quiet lake. Or the high-pitched hum of that one last mosquito you failed to get out of the tent at zip-up time.

*   *   *

Our spiritual need of food and fellowship, our intellectual need to know and grow, our creative need to make and enjoy beautiful things, and our psychological need for security and "unwinding" through recreation are all needs known to our Heavenly Father. He is aware of our needs, as we should also be. Whatever our standard of living, He can help us to creatively design patterns by which we can meet these needs for ourselves and our families.

Chapter Ten

Putting Things in Place

It was just before Christmas. Cam and I were finishing up a bit of shopping at a large city mall. We had done a lot more looking than buying, with very little money in our pockets. As we stepped outside, I noticed an elegant woman drive up to the parcel delivery depot in a big white sedan. Her strawberry-blond hair was beautifully swirled, her makeup meticulous. I couldn't help but smile to myself at the obvious contrast between her economic condition and mine.

Then, as the young woman, wrapped in a luxurious fur, stepped out of the car to give directions to the boy carrying out her parcels, our eyes met, and we gasped with the shock of instant recognition.

"Peggy!"

"Maxine!"

She was a high school girlfriend with whom I had long since lost contact. We stood together on the sidewalk, chatting eagerly about the years that had intervened between high school and this moment. Peggy had done secretarial work in several large cities; then she had married a lawyer. "I'm so glad things have gone so well for you, Peggy," I told her.

"And how about you?" she asked. The physical realities of our situation were, at that moment, almost painfully apparent—I wearing a much-worn leather coat over a cotton dress and Cam in old jeans. "Well," I said, "we're trying to get started in farming, and our youngest child is just nine months old."

"Your youngest?" Peggy asked. "You have how many?"

"Four," I said. "Two girls and two boys. They're beautiful."

A shadow went across her eyes. "You lucky thing," she said. "We still don't have any. But we're hoping."

As she slipped back into her big, beautiful car, I waved good-bye and walked across the parking lot to our current second-hand car wondering which of two classmates was really the richer.

A friend of ours who also lost very heavily in the cattle business reversal that dumped us overboard told us, "My men keep asking me why I'm smiling. And I just have to tell them that if I'm healthy in body and relatively stable in mind — and if on top of that I have life in my spirit through faith in the Lord Jesus Christ — then, man! No matter how much money I may have lost, I am still a wealthy man!"

Defining "Poverty" and "Wealth"
What is poverty? What is wealth? No field could possibly be more relative than this. Today, of course, we are helped in our definition of poverty by the annual statement of government offices concerning the "poverty line." Radio announcers and newspaper writers grab up the releases from our economic councils. We read it; we hear it: "Any family of 3.7 with a net earning of less than $XY,000 per annum is living — officially — below the poverty line."

We did not know about the poverty line when we were kids. Looking back to our childhood, my brother once exclaimed, "We were poor, but we never knew it." Poor we may have been — poverty-stricken we were not. We had all the best of everything that really mattered. With good and godly parents, lovingly providing for far more than our physical needs while building a modest family home quite literally over our heads with their own hands, we children were anything but poor. Our personalities were sustained by love and encouragement; our minds stimulated by exposure to ideas, books, and interesting people; our spirits nurtured by the Bible, daily read and taught, and—more important—interpreted into life by our parents. When I go back to the city of Lethbridge and drive nostalgically down Twelfth Avenue South past the house where my earliest "little girl" memories took place, I am always surprised to see how small the house and yard are. By today's standards, our home was tiny. But to four growing children, it was home. We lived in the basement while our parents built the upstairs. And when the upstairs was completed and we "moved up," what joy! Our living area was doubled overnight. And we counted ourselves "kings of infinite space."

Today, it is much harder for families to keep the simple joy of not *feeling* poor. Having conducted a poll concerning attitudes toward poverty and riches, Martin Goldfarb in a *Reader's Digest* article concluded: "Poverty . . . is more than a physical thing; it's more than being deprived of dollars; it is an attitude, a sense of defeat, a loss of dignity."[1] For this very reason, government enunciations of the "poverty line" are misleading at best and, at worst, may be damaging. It is one thing to be poor. It is quite another to be told you are poor.

It is hard to work out a clear idea of relative poverty and relative wealth. Between the government telling us at what income we are poor or underprivileged, and the television presenting dramas on palatial show-home sets, it is hard to get a balanced idea of what real poverty or real wealth consists. Perhaps we have to turn to history, to read of the discomforts experienced by even the wealthy of two or three centuries ago, in order to understand the wealth we have in what we consider to be just ordinary, accepted comforts. Perhaps we have to come to terms with the housing conditions of the average peasant of the Middle Ages. Or really get an understanding of how the *average* person in many areas of our world lives today. Perhaps we need to go without a meal or two to find out what hunger really feels like. There are standards by which all of us, even the most pressed, are actually wealthy. There is a sense in which feeling "poor" or "rich" depends only upon to whose condition you compare your own.

There is, of course, such a thing as poverty. Real poverty. It is a miserable state of grinding necessity. When there is unremitting pressure in trying to make an income go around necessities — food, clothing, housing, and transportation — then there is, indeed, poverty. And poverty has its negative effect. It distorts the value of money. "More money" becomes very important. A person begins to dream of windfalls. And materialism becomes just as real a problem to the family which is truly experiencing poverty as it is to the very rich who also might be dominated by thoughts of material things. Or more so.

I remember how I gazed at those "Win a Dream Home" sweepstake advertisements that came our way — with chances to win (about one in ten million) based on buying anything from magazine subscriptions to face cream. Never had tickets for raffles had such drawing power; never before or since have I been so tempted to buy lottery tickets. In the end, we got our dream home — or at least a simplified version of it, in the way we were intended to: by praying and working and planning; by borrowing and repaying. But the experience of the power of *wish* during a time of deprivation gave me a deep sympathy for the many poor who become addicted to bingo and other games of chance; having lost hope in their ability to improve their circumstances, they cling to the hope of a windfall. I have also become deeply angry at governments that supplement tax revenue by lotteries. Because it is the poor who are most susceptible to the hope of a win, public lotteries amount to a form of taxation on the wistful hopes of the poor.

But physical, lack-of-money poverty is really only one aspect of the kind of impoverishment which cripples the human spirit and hampers the total growth of the individual. We need to develop discernment in a number of areas if we are ever to be released to enjoy the riches we may already have and are not recognizing as such.

First, to understand what state constitutes wealth and what constitutes poverty, we must distinguish between the temporal and the eternal. It is important for us as Christians to live in this present world in the light of the eternal one. The things of this life, no matter how good or how many, are only beloved trappings of a temporary earthly existence. Real riches must be spiritual riches, things which will outlast this earthly existence. This is what Jesus taught in Matthew 6:19-24; it is reiterated throughout the New Testament.

The physical is so immediate to us — as pressing as our own skins — and because it is proclaimed by so many forces which press physical and material needs and wants upon us, we may forget where our real interests lie. As believers in the resurrected Christ, who has pioneered the way into eternal life for us (see Heb. 6:19-20), we sense a reality beyond this life. The richest people in the world are those who are aware of the spiritual, eternal dimension of life into which we enter by faith. These people know that the real things are the things that cannot be seen with the eye.

Writing instructions to a junior devil on how to tempt a new Christian away from discipleship to Christ, "Screwtape" says:

> The sense of ownership in general is always to be encouraged. The humans are always putting up claims to ownership which sound equally funny in Heaven and in Hell and we must keep them doing so. . . . We produce this sense of ownership not only by pride but by confusion. We teach them not to notice the different sense of the possessive pronoun — the finely graded differences that run from "my boots" . . . to "my God."[2]

Let's face it: real poverty is the lot of every one of us — from those who work hard at wrapping inadequate incomes around the needs of a family to those who have so much that they are bored — if and when material things are first, and when this temporal world is treated as most important. Real poverty is the burning desire to possess, to claim more and more things as "mine." From this need to possess stems all sorts of contentions (see James 4:2-3). From this need to possess comes the continuous and much-encouraged breaking of the tenth commandment: "You shall not covet" (Exodus 20:17). From this need to possess comes our unending greed.

In a well-known essay on "The Blessedness of Possessing Nothing," Tozer describes the craving to possess as "a tough, fibrous root of fallen life whose nature is to possess, always to possess." He says:

> The way to deeper knowledge of God is through the lonely valley of soul poverty and abnegation of all things. The blessed ones who possess the Kingdom are they who have repudiated every external thing and have rooted from their hearts all sense of possessing. . . . These blessed poor are no longer slaves to the tyranny of things.[3]

Another distinction we need to learn to make is between those things we need for physical survival in this temporal world and those things we merely crave in order to boost sagging egos, to confirm our identities somehow, or to project a success image. Joy Duncan, a writer friend of mine, commented in a letter to me:

> People . . . suffer these days from a lack of identity. So many are caught in unrewarding jobs without the struggle and sense of direction our pioneers had simply to stay alive. It's a willy-nilly kind of existence. So they compensate by striving for *things* — "I know who I am now. I'm the owner of a new car." "Look at me. I'm somebody because the neighbors come to swim in my pool." It's a basic lack of self-worth that is alleviated by comparing oneself, favorably, with others — and, of course, if you can't compete in the "things" sweepstakes or don't measure up, it is devastating. It would be so simple if people would believe in themselves — which, as you point out, is a spiritual thing. If we are important to God, what else can matter?

We need too to distinguish between real faith in God and a mere faith in things. Turning Christianity into a "faith in God for things" is a sad, materialistic travesty of the Gospel which has rooted itself stubbornly in our consciousness.

A favorite hymn of mine says:

> My goal is God Himself, not joy, nor peace,
> Nor even blessing, but Himself, my God.[4]

But I still find the words easier to sing than really to live. Yet, finally, it is only as we get caught up in this larger vision — this possibility of intimacy with our Creator, a terrifying and purifying thought, that we can set down our preoccupying toys and direct our energies toward loving and knowing and bringing joy to the heart of the One "who loved me, and gave Himself for me" (Gal. 2:20).

Real poverty must be ultimately described in spiritual terms. It is to be "without hope and without God in the world" (Eph. 2:12). It was this kind of poverty that Jesus came to eradicate. Certainly He was concerned about physical needs. He fed the hungry. He healed the sick. And all without charge. He lived the simple life and shared all that He had and was with others. But over and over again, He pointed out that the deep need of the soul could never be satisfied with bread alone. It is as we recognize the inner emptiness of our spirits and come to Him that He meets our deepest needs. He fills our hunger with the living bread. He satisfies our thirst with the living water. He supplants our cravings for "things" with Himself.

Real poverty is to be without Christ. Or, having made a profession of salvation, not to find our existence saturated and blessed by His presence. Real poverty is to want things — anything — more than we want God. Real poverty is to have our lives cluttered, the good seed of God's Word "choked by life's worries, riches and pleasures" of this life and fail to bring any fruit to maturity (Luke 8:14).

Ultimately, we can conclude that real poverty is a state of mind in which *things* are uppermost. Real poverty is when hunger pangs force from my mind all thoughts but those of food. Real poverty is when the children are not dressed warmly enough for winter. Real poverty is when the housing we can afford is not adequate to the needs of our families. On the other hand, real poverty is—equally—when I have eaten so much that I am uncomfortable, and again, my thoughts center on food. Or when I have so many clothes that I have to spend a lot of mental energy making choices among them or finding ways to store them. Or when, regardless of my living conditions, I am discontent and brooding about how to have more. Real poverty is when material things are uppermost and pressing—whether because we have too few or too many of them. It is poverty, because the human mind and spirit are made for higher things, worthier pursuits. As Barbara, a teenager in a girls' group I led, wrote:

> Like a bird, I soar
> Heavenward, My spirit free—
> Earth pulls me down.

When earth pulls us down, we are poor.

There is, however, a kind of poverty that Jesus called "blessed." He did not call it blessed to be cold or hungry or homeless (and everywhere in the New Testament, the writers take it for granted that as Christians we must do all we can to alleviate that kind of poverty). But Jesus called it blessed to be "poor in spirit" (Matt. 5:3). Actually, we are all poor in spirit. Spiritual poverty is our legacy. But Jesus calls us "happy" or "blessed" when we recognize our spiritual bankruptcy and turn to Him.

In the last book of the Bible, God's revelation given to John addressed to two different churches gives us insight into the real meaning of poverty and riches—not as seen from our own time-bound and thing-counting point of view, but from God's. To the church in Smyrna, the Spirit directs a kindly message: "I know your afflictions and your poverty—yet you are rich" (Rev. 2:9). Here, a church which was suffering persecution and physical poverty was warmly reminded of its real riches. Rich in the kingdom of heaven, where it really matters.

There is an entirely different tone in the message the Spirit directs to the church of Laodicea: "You say, 'I am rich . . . and do not need a thing.' But you do not realize that you are wretched, pitiful, poor, blind and naked" (Rev. 3:17-19). To be spiritually bankrupt and physically rich was the great problem of that church, and the tragedy of many of us who are believers today, especially in the affluent West. In that kind of poverty — that tragic, abject poverty which passes as wealth — there is no blessedness. To the poor-rich church at Smyrna, the Spirit says a word of encouragement: "Be faithful, even to the point of death, and I will give you the crown of life" (2:10). But to the rich-poor church in Laodicea, His word is admonishment: "I counsel you to buy from me gold refined in fire, so you can become rich" (3:18). Could it be that He was directing the church to ask for testing, for persecution, for adversity, in order to "melt down" the riches that the world can see in exchange for the true riches of having been faithful in testing?

These letters in Revelation summarize a tension that is felt in many of the epistles of the New Testament: the continual danger of mistaking "gain" for "godliness." Paul warns Timothy about "men of corrupt mind . . . who think that godliness is a means to financial gain." And then he spells it out: "But godliness with contentment is great gain" (1 Tim. 6:6).

Godliness — What Is It?
Godliness. What a strange, old-fashioned word that is, almost as remote as "holiness." We recognize it as a church word, a Bible word. But what does it look like in everyday clothes?

If "godliness" conjures images of long meetings with men preaching and women wearing buns, we probably need to consider what it really is: a life that is God-centered and growing toward God; a life in which the Holy Spirit is restoring the damaged and dented image of God so that in our priorities and attitudes and outlook we can be seen to be becoming more and more like the One who made — and remakes — us.

It consists, first of all, in having spiritual life, life that comes from God. We are born spiritually bankrupt, spiritually dead (Eph. 2:1). And only as we receive the vitality of the living Christ into our lives by faith can we experience what Jesus called the "new birth" (see John 3:1-18). Godliness begins with spiritual birth. But it does not stop there.

Godliness is seeing things as God does: The things of this world as good in that they add comfort to our short stay on this earth, but as secondary in importance to the ultimately real things which are spiritual and eternal; the things of this world as loaned only as a trust for which we will be called to give account. Godliness is using the good things of this life as God would, as a means of bringing blessing to others.

Paul outlined three reasons for diligence in business:

• To be able to pay our debts and live honestly (Eph. 4:28; 1 Thes. 4:11-12);
• To provide for ourselves and our own families (1 Thes. 4:11-12; 1 Tim. 5:8);
• To share with those who are less fortunate (Eph. 4:28).
These are goals consistent with a godly attitude toward things.

If we really claim to be children of God through faith in Jesus Christ, then the first quest of our lives must be godliness. We can only develop godliness, or a godly perspective on things, as we deepen our devotional life, as we read the Word of God daily and soak up what the Bible reveals about ourselves and about our God. And we will always be challenged in our quest for godliness by that standard set by our Lord Jesus Himself: "Be perfect, therefore, even as your heavenly Father which is in heaven is perfect" (Matt. 5:48).

Whenever "things" become central in our lives, whether legitimate in themselves or not, then—if we are truly children of God—we can expect that His Holy Spirit will bring pressures to bear to move those things out of the center of our hearts and thoughts, out to the periphery where they belong. For the center of our beings must belong to God alone.

And then, going back to Paul's phrase describing "great gain," godliness is to be with contentment.

How to Find Contentment
Contentment is the key to the restful, rejoicing Christian life. Godliness first. And then, with God at the center of our lives, contentment follows. Things become only as important as they should be: necessary to sustain physical life, but not necessary to build up our egos or to maintain a special status. As we mature in our walk with our Lord, things should lose their luster and their appeal. Certainly, the more time we spend looking into the face of Jesus in devotional worship, the less interest the things of this world will hold for us.

In a recent phone call, my friend Donna told me, "Oh, Jerry thought about taking an extra job this winter, when the farming's a bit slack, so that we could finish up our basement. But I talked him out of it. You know, a few years ago that would have seemed mighty important to me. But now I know that the time we spend together as a family is far more important than wallboard on the rumpus room. It's funny how you get weaned from things, isn't it?"

I knew exactly what she meant. When we first thought we might be able to build a house, the idea consumed me. I spent hours making sketches, studying plans, scanning home magazines. And the Lord removed the possibility of building at that time. Later, with house plans again on the kitchen table, I found that I was interested only in making good and wise choices. The house had ceased to be a thing of importance in itself; it was now a means to the end of fulfilling our responsibilities to our growing children and of being settled so that we could serve the Lord effectively in the ministries He had entrusted to us.

*   *   *

When we know the basic provision of day-by-day needs, claiming by faith our daily bread; when we have healthy and secure children; and when we experience love and joy in our relationships with others, both within and outside of the home, then we are really rich. And when we live in relationship with God as our Father through faith in Christ, made real by the Holy Spirit, we are in fellowship with the whole awesome Trinity, and our wealth is beyond all reckoning.

The good life, as I see it, is the uncluttered life, the life in which the main goals are spiritual, the life in which the main riches are eternal. If along the way God should entrust to our care physical goods as well, then that is a responsibility just as much as a privilege. We need to be prodded into remembering that real security can never be found "in wealth, which is so uncertain," and so put [our] hope in God" (1 Tim. 6:17).

- Real poverty is to depend on things for identity or status.
- Real wealth is to find our true worth in the love of Jesus Christ.

- Real poverty is to depend on things for security or for happiness.
- Real wealth is to come to God for these things which only fellowship with Him can bring into our lives.

- Real poverty is to be thing-dominated in our daily lives.
- Real wealth is to have our lives centered on the Lord Jesus Christ.

- Real poverty is to make all the investments of our lives in material things.
- Real wealth is to make our primary investment in knowing God and serving others.

- Real poverty is to live in fear and insecurity in changing times.
- Real wealth is to know that, ultimately, our only security is God Himself and His promise of safe passage into His presence.

The good life is not one which can be defined as being above any arbitrary poverty line. It is, simply, "godliness with contentment." It is simplicity with dignity. It is having without holding. And that is — not only now, but ultimately — "great gain."

Chapter Eleven

Where We're at — and Where We're Going

Some years ago, I sat in the shade of the historical reconstruction of the fur-trading fort from which the city of Edmonton has grown and chatted with an historian, Dr. J.G. MacGregor, about conditions, past and present. A regional writer, he had himself lived through enormous changes here in western Canada. He spent his first winter in Canada in a tent, something which those of us who survive our bitter winters in warm houses find almost unimaginable. "Things will change back," he said. "It is inevitable. I don't think they will get as hard as they were for the early pioneers. But nowadays a young woman thinks nothing of going downtown and buying a new dress every other week. In the old days, it was an event to get new clothing once a year. And it will go back to that. I predict that before long the economy will be slowed down to that extent. And let's face it," he added thoughtfully, "it won't be all for the bad."

Those of us who read our Bibles know that Dr. MacGregor is no doubt right. Widespread economic chaos and famine are predicted in the Book of Revelation. Both are now upon our world. But surely this is not a time for Christians to go about with worried frowns, clutching frantically at our diminishing consumer power.

Looking Ahead

More recently, I talked with Dr. Bruce Wilkinson, a professor of international economics at the University of Alberta. He feels the outlook for the next two decades may be very grim, especially for a country like Canada with high international debt, but perhaps for other Western nations as well. Feeling that there will not be much relief from human suffering from governments which have already overspent, or from multinational corporations with little concern for the local populace, Dr. Wilkinson expects changes that will remind us that, biblically, the essential economic unit is the family. "Families will have to look after their own," he says. "And, furthermore, we will have to relearn how to interpret family not only in terms of our immediate kin, but in the larger sense of the church community."

Indicators already exist to show that income distribution both within individual Western economies and between nations is becoming less equitable with an increasing concentration of people at both ends: the highly wealthy and the desperately poor no longer buffered by a large middle class. Many futurists see this inequity as contributing not only to personal, but to global, insecurity. But, of course, attempts at redistribution may well lower the standard of living and eat into the security we have established for ourselves.

It is not, however, a time to wring our hands or to live in despair. Building a renewed sense of responsibility for each other into family and redeveloping a sense of local community — within the church and within a particular geographic locale — may be, finally, the best means of securing our futures. As we are obedient to God, we will rediscover what His people have always known: that ultimately, God — rather than our bank accounts or retirement plans or even our family or community — is our security. As we seek to live in obedience to Him, we can look to Him for His promised provision. Isaiah, speaking to a people of God in times of international instability, saw that God desired action, not just religious piety. Isaiah challenged them to consider that God's kind of "fast" or religious observance is:

> To loose the chain of injustice
>   and untie the cords of the yoke,
> to set the oppressed free
>   and break every yoke . . .
> to share your food with the hungry
>   and to provide the poor wanderer with shelter —
> when you see the naked, to clothe him,
>   and not to turn away from your own flesh and blood
> (Isa. 58:6-7).

And when God's people obey, and live out principles of justice and compassion — at the family and community level as a starting point, but with an awareness of the larger international community as well, God's promise is clear:

> Then your light will break forth like the dawn,
>   and your healing will quickly appear. . . .
> Then you will call, and the Lord will answer;
>   you will cry for help, and He will say,
>   Here am I (58:8-9).

Despite seeing a pretty grim economic prospect, Dr. Wilkinson feels that Christians should not be living in fear. "We should praise God even at times of economic uncertainty because God is in control. We can live in peace, joyful that we can be alive at this time and that He has given us the privilege of having a little part in His great play."

The call to reconsideration of our lifestyle is being pressed upon us by a number of economic facts: recessions, inflation, the pressing needs of the Third World. It is a call which is being issued by politicians as well as preachers. It is a time, if not for sacrifice, at least for restraint. But it was our Lord Himself who issued a far wider call almost two millennia ago:

> Do not store up for yourselves treasures on earth,
> where moth and rust destroy, and where thieves break
> in and steal. But store up for yourselves treasures in

heaven, . . . for where your treasure is, there will your
heart be also. . . . You cannot serve God and riches
(Matt. 6:19-21, 24).

A Glance Back
A few years ago the call for restraint was neither so pressing
nor quite so inescapable. For the Christian young person growing up when I did, there seemed to be two main vocations or
callings. One was to "full-time service," which meant limited
income, but presumably adequate rewards in nonmaterial
terms. The other equally honorable calling was to enter a career of your choice and, with any luck at all, to get rich. Not
necessarily really wealthy, mind you. But by any global standard comparison, rich. The Christian press was turning out a
spate of "success stories" for an eager, but not always percep-
tive, audience which gradually came to equate riches with righteousness, and financial acumen with faith. The super-success-
ful businessman or professional person was promoted as the
image of the *average,* or at least the *normal* Christian.

It all added up to a prevailing feeling that anyone who didn't
"make it," on the same standard of success which the world
around us used, was somehow a second-class citizen not only in
society as a whole, but in the Church of Jesus Christ as well. The
"gold-ring principle," whereby the "man . . . in goodly apparel"
had obvious preferment within the church (see James 2:1-10),
became an obvious feature of our evangelical churches.

Of course, this development can be given a broader historical setting. By doing so, we can help ourselves understand the
assumptions on which we have built our value structures,
structures which now, in the white light of the "present dis-
tress" seem to be so inadequate and so unscriptural.

First of all, there is the immediate historical context. My
parents' generation lived through the Great Depression. The
"dirty thirties" left an imprint on the mind of every person
who passed through them, an ineradicable memory of pressing
poverty which created a desire for things: not just for things in
themselves, but for things as an indication of security. People

who lived through those days wanted to be sure that they themselves would never know that kind of pressure again, and to be certain that their children would not have to go through such an experience of poverty. Making money, saving money, and buying things assumed an importance out of all proportion to needs in the shadow of the great want of the 1930s.

The same phenomenon has been seen in immigrants who came to North America in the wake of the European holocaust of World War II. In high school days, I had a friend who with her parents had lived in refugee camps after the war. She still spoke with a heavy accent, and even then her eyes had the haunted look of a child who had known hunger and cold and fear. I found her family, a Christian family, astonishing in its continuous talk and thought of "things." The accumulation of things seemed to obsess every waking hour for every family member. And, of course, with thrift and hard work, they were catching up quickly with their neighbors in material possessions. Such aggressive acquisitiveness cannot be criticized without a sympathetic understanding of its psychological basis.

A second fairly immediate historical aspect of our acceptance of wealth as a worthy goal in life lies in the history of the evangelical movement itself. This movement, and especially that part of it which in North America has been known as "fundamentalism," has been largely a movement of the poor and of the uneducated. And when any semi-outcast group begins to become socially acceptable, a very strong emphasis is placed on those things which bring upward mobility and respectability: education and wealth. Thus, in our conservative evangelical circles, we have in recent years tended to exalt those persons who are better educated and those who are more wealthy as the leaders who can bring us acceptance in our larger society.

These historical and sociological factors help us understand how the "company of the redeemed," named for a Man who had "no place to lay His head," has become a "company of the rich," (Matt. 8:20) or at least a company of people who look on riches as a seal of God's approval and as a worthwhile goal in life.

As we search out our roots deeper in history, we find that many major historians have seen links between the theology of the Protestant Reformation and the rise of capitalism. The Weber thesis, proposed soon after the turn of the century, has made a major impact on historical thought. Weber proposed that the "spirit of capitalism" had appeared in history as a result or by-product of the religious ethic of Calvinism.[1] R.H. Tawney's *Religion and the Rise of Capitalism* was both a refinement and a popularization of the Weber thesis. And while a causal link between Protestantism and capitalism is difficult to forge in a way that is utterly convincing, it has not been hard for scholars to see that the two movements, one spiritual and the other economic, have made good traveling companions. Many of the cause-effect historians who have followed in the Weber tradition have been hostile both to Protestantism and to capitalism, which certainly taints the objectivity of their work. But it is possible for us to learn from even hostile critics, and Tawney's biting comment is worth pondering:

> To countless generations of religious thinkers, the fundamental maxim of Christian social ethics had seemed to be expressed in the words of St. Paul to Timothy: "Having food and raiment, let us be therewith content. For the love of money is the root of all evil." Now [after the Reformation] . . . not sufficiency to the needs of daily life, but limitless increase and expansion, became the goal of the Christian's efforts. . . . Plunged in the cleansing waters of later Puritanism, the qualities which less enlightened ages had denounced as social vices emerged as economic virtues.[2]

The great Wesleyan revival of the eighteenth century is credited by historians as providing an all-important "brake for the un-trammelled self-interest of individuals pursuing the ends of their personal and private gain."[3] Yet John Wesley himself, as an old man, warned:

The Methodists in every place grow diligent and frugal; consequently, they increase in goods. Hence, they proportionably increase in pride, in anger, in the desire of the flesh, the desire of the eyes, and the pride of life. So, although the form of religion remains, the spirit is swiftly vanishing away.[4]

Reconsidering Our Values

It is important for us to understand on what foundations our traditions and assumptions rest. It is significant for us to discover just where we are at.

To those of us who grew up in the affluent post-war period in North America, the value of money was well taught. Christianity and the accumulation of capital seemed not only compatible, but causally linked together.

Now, however, we find ourselves living in a world for which we feel strangely unprepared. The goal of business success at any cost and the sometimes questionable profit-making no longer seem to be satisfactory as an expression of a Christian life view. We live in a world in which other goals and a broader ethic are required, not only for personal spiritual survival, but for national economic survival and for global physical survival. Business must thrive for people to have both work to do and income to make decisions about. But maximization of profit has to be balanced with ethical concern for the conditions in which people work and the impact of the process of production and the end-products themselves on the community and the environment.

More and more, people at all levels of our society are talking about a closed economy. While political leaders urge restraint, a bearded postal worker, involved against his own better judgment in a prolonged strike, says to a television interviewer: "Sure, I'd like to have more of the pie. But I guess we've all got to realize that there is only so much pie." The message is getting through. Only so much pie and the necessity of sharing it equitably: that is the greatest economic and social problem of our day. Only so much fuel, and how it should be apportioned.

Only so much air, and how it can be kept breathable.

The world economy, which became apparently endlessly capable of expansion through the discovery of half a world in the fifteenth and sixteenth centuries, and the industrial revolution of the eighteenth and nineteenth centuries, has suddenly snapped shut again. And we feel trapped in this closure. We find ourselves like the peasants in a medieval village, suddenly members of a vast "global village" in which many feel that we are, indeed, "our brothers' keepers." We know now that nonrenewable resources can be exhausted. We, as individuals and as nations, are aware that there is such a thing as debt becoming due and payable.

We sit in our living rooms and look into the "unseeing eye" of our television sets and see not just individuals but entire cities and nations going bankrupt. And at the same time we look into the empty eyes of swollen-bellied children of famine who are somehow, impossibly, still alive. And we know that somewhere, in some way, we are all personally responsible. But just sitting around with vague guilt feelings haunting us is hardly a sufficient response. We need to seriously reevaluate our whole set of life goals and to ask ourselves, "Where are we now? And where are we going?" We must put to ourselves the question: "Is my lifestyle supporting a famine somewhere in the world today?" We need to get back to our New Testaments to discover how truly Christian principles, enunciated by the Lord Jesus Himself and exemplified by the first-century Christians, can help lead the way in reaching out to others in our world.

If we are, indeed, not content to sit back and wait in helplessness for the waves of present and future shock to overwhelm us," we need to become actively involved in adjusting our goals, expanding our ethic, and moderating our lifestyle to meet the needs of this changing age. As believers in the Lord Jesus Christ, "we do not belong to the night or to the darkness. So then . . . let us be alert and self-controlled" (1 Thes. 5:6).

As we study the New Testament, we understand that one of the exciting things about the attempt to bring our lives back

into line with the scriptural plumb line is that Christian principles are workable in any economic structure. The New Testament does not prescribe an economic system, nor does it endorse any particular economic theories. What it does do is tell
the believer how to operate within whatever economic structure, or stricture, he finds himself. And how, in the light of
biblical principles of justice and compassion, to critique and
work for the improvement of the system in which we find
ourselves.

Any cinching in of our belts that we undertake will not, in
the long run, hurt any of us. It is very often only when we
begin to feel pinched economically that we start to sort out the
debris of our things-cluttered lives and decide which things are
really important and which are peripheral.

Responding to Change

As citizens of a global village, a hungry global village, and as
people who believe we will give account to our returning Lord for
how we have lived, we must respond to the very obvious needs
of others. Not just intuitively, sympathetically, or guiltily, but
thoughtfully and philosophically, with a firm basis in the guidelines of the Scriptures, so that we can act boldly and with
conviction and not merely react to things as they happen. We
must, as those who bear the name of the compassionate Jesus,
exercise leadership in finding better ways to share with others.
We must take our cue from the Lord Jesus Christ Himself and
get a correct valuation on the things of this world.

Many years have passed since Paul wrote this warning:
"From now on those . . . who buy something [should live] as if
it were not theirs to keep; those who use the things of the
world, as if not engrossed in them. For this world in its
present form is passing away" (1 Cor. 7:29-31).

If the time was short then, it is obviously far shorter now.
As Christians, we dare not sit around, rendered helpless by
"future shock." Instead, we need to be quick to adapt to the
new economic and social realities of our world, quick to respond lovingly to the needs of others.

We live in urgent days, and our time of opportunity to share the Gospel, to share the good things of this world, may be very short. We need to live as people whose lives might be suddenly cut off. We need to learn, and we could learn from the Scriptures if we would come to them, the lessons that Aleksandr Solzhenitsyn learned through his experience of *The Gulag Archipelago:*

> What about the main thing in life, all its riddles? If you want, I'll spell it out for you right now. Do not pursue what is illusory—property and position: all that is gained at the expense of your nerves decade after decade, and is confiscated one fell night. Live with a steady superiority over life—don't be afraid of misfortune and do not yearn after happiness. . . . Our envy of others devours us most of all. Rub your eyes and purify your heart—and prize above all else in the world those who love you and wish you well.[5]

Seven years of Soviet prison camp and many more years of listening to the stories of hundreds of other prisoners taught Solzhenitsyn this truth, one which a child could learn from the Gospels, but one which we adults often tend to forget.

That the dark days detailed in the Book of Revelation are soon to break about this earth is all too clear. In an interview filmed before his death, historian Arnold Toynbee raised this question:

> Will man draw on the spiritual resources available from beyond himself—or not? On the answer to that question hinges the future of humanity—if there is to be one.[6]

It is no longer just the funny little man declaring, "The end is at hand." It's just that he knew it first.

So this is a time for uncluttered, tidied-up Christian living. Because the Lord is "patient . . . not wanting anyone to perish, but everyone to come to repentance" (2 Peter 3:9), there may yet be some time before the end. But events are inexorably bringing us closer to the return of Jesus Christ.

Living in Hope

If we do, indeed, live in the last days before the return of Jesus Christ, we are living close to the consummation of the great purifying hope of the church. Believers throughout the ages have lived in anticipation of the return of Jesus Christ, and the implication of the imminence of that return has always been to ask, "What kind of people ought [we] to be?" With the answer being: "You ought to live holy and godly lives as you look forward to the day of God and speed its coming" (2 Peter 3:11-12).

We can have the quiet confidence which Jesus intended to be the distinguishing mark of His disciples in the face of troubled times: We can obey His command to "lift up your heads, because your redemption is drawing near" (Luke 21:28) if, first of all, we are sure that we are His.

I remember once thinking about the return of my Lord and Savior, and being troubled by the thought: "When He comes, will I know Him? He is One whom I have loved, sight unseen. I have only artists' conceptions on which to base any visualization of the Lord Jesus Christ." And then the Lord brought to my mind the verse of Scripture, "He calls His own sheep by name and leads them out" (John 10:3). I realized, with a great sense of relief, that the important question was not so much, "Will I know Him?" but rather, "Will He know me?" For since I am one of His sheep, He will call me by name. What a restful confidence.

The Apostle Peter invites us to "be all the more eager to make your calling and election sure" (2 Peter 1:10), to take time to ascertain that we are, without doubt, participants in God's plan of redemption. And the Apostle John, in his first epistle, tells us the tests by which we can validate our personal positions relative to Jesus Christ. You may wish to study that letter in detail for yourself, but I see there these three main tests by which we can examine our claims to saving faith:

1. *The test of confession of sin (1 John 1:5-10).* If we try to lay claim to having done the best we could, or having lived as well as the next guy, as our basis for entering God's family, we "deceive ourselves." There is only one way in which we can know the cleansing that is necessary to make us acceptable in God's sight, and that is through confession and turning from sin. If we have confessed our sins and thus experienced forgiveness and cleansing, we have passed John's first test. If not, then this is the starting point. We can feel nothing but fear at the thought of Christ's return until we have cried out, "God have mercy on me, a sinner" (Luke 18:13).

2. *The test of obedience to our new Master (1 John 2:3-8).* Confession of sin is certainly the first step, but it is not the only one. John points out that we can know that we know Christ "if we obey His commandments" (v. 3). If we are changed persons because we live under new management, then we can face the visible, personal return of that Master, Jesus Christ, with confidence. Obedience to Christ will have two very distinct effects, as John points out:

• *Love (1 John 2:9-11).* Obedience to Christ as Lord and Master must result in an attitude of love toward our Christian brothers and sisters as well as toward those in the broader brotherhood of humanity (3:14-19). This kind of love has inescapable economic implications!

• *Right living (3:6-10).* Christ cannot be in control of a life without creating righteousness, or right living, in that individual. John is unsparing here. If we claim to have confessed our sins and thus to have entered into salvation, and then go on sinning, we're fooling only ourselves. As we abide in Christ and let His Holy Spirit give us power and direction for right living, we know "that when He appears we may be confident and unashamed before Him at His coming" (2:28). Not that we never again sin after our initial confession, but that we do not continue sinning: this is the important thought here.

Again, we need to ask ourselves: "Do our lives pass the test of obedience?" If not, perhaps we have never come to a point of decisively turning over our lives to the lordship of Jesus Christ. We need to reach the point where we cry out to the Lord as Saul did on the Damascus road (see Acts 9). When we do, because He is Lord, He will begin to bring our lives into conformity with His life. And we can look forward to His return with joyful confidence.

3. *The test of right doctrine concerning Jesus Christ (1 John 4:1-4).* John makes it very clear that what we think and say of Jesus Christ is very important. After Jesus' ascension, the angelic witness was that "this same Jesus" would return (Acts 1:11). We need to reexamine the scriptural evidence concerning the nature and person of Jesus Christ; we need to assure ourselves that we are, indeed, awaiting "this same Jesus." Not some nameless force for good, not some mysterious other manifestation, not just the kingdom of God on earth in demonstrations of love and peace among men, but "this same Jesus." The same Jesus who was born at Bethlehem, God in human flesh; who was heard and seen and known in Galilee, the Living Word; who was crucified outside of Jerusalem as the Lamb of God, the ultimate sacrifice for man's sin; who was raised from death, all His amazing claims fully vindicated in one act of enormous triumph. *This,* and no other, is the Jesus who will return in power. To be awaiting some other is to become vulnerable to the "false Christs" who, Jesus warned His disciples, would come before His own return.

Since God has ordained salvation only through His Son, Jesus Christ, right doctrine concerning Him is essential to any true experience of salvation—any experience that will pass the test.

Having set out these three crucial tests, John holds out this hope of perfect confidence to the believer: "I write these things . . . that you may *know* that you have eternal life" (1 John 5:13, emphasis mine).

We do not need to have our anticipation of Christ's return chilled by a tremor of fear if we have made sure of our relationship to Him. We can have further confidence as we look ahead if we know that our hearts are full of love for Jesus our

Lord, if we are learning to be untrammeled by affections and desires that bind us to this temporal world.

It is in the confidence of Christ's return that we face a threatening future. It is in the confidence that we are His that we embrace and declare this glad hope. And it is in the light of this that we affirm our position as "aliens and strangers on earth" (Heb. 11:13). Occupied with the day-to-day tasks of earning a living and making a home, concerned with the responsible conserving and sharing of this world's goods, we nonetheless live in the glad expectancy of His return: Maranatha! Come, O Lord!

Notes

CHAPTER 1: THE CALL TO MODEST LIVING
1. Francis Schaeffer, *Pollution and the Death of Man: the Christian View of Ecology* (Wheaton: Tyndale, 1972), 85.

CHAPTER 2: THE GOLDEN MEAN
1. Stanley Tam, *God Owns My Business* (Waco: Word, 1969), 112.
2. Harold J. Sutton, "Immortal Money: A Study of Tithing," *Alliance Witness*, 17 March 1965, 5.

CHAPTER 3: CONTENTMENT: LEARNED, NOT EARNED
1. David Grayson, *Adventures in Contentment* (New York: Grosset and Dunlap, 1906), 3.
2. Ibid., 5.

CHAPTER 4: LIVING ON LOVE
1. Catherine S. Chilman, Fred M. Cox, Elam W. Nunnally, *Employment and Economic Problems*, Families in Trouble Series, vol. 1 (Newbury Park: Sage, 1988) 46–48, 74–76.
2. Ibid., 46.

CHAPTER 5: STOPPING THE MERRY-GO-ROUND
1. Robert Schuller, *Move Ahead with Possibility Thinking* (Old Tappan: Revell, 1973), 107.
2. "A Way to Keep Your Debts Under Control," *Changing Times*, February 1969.

CHAPTER 6: BASIC NEEDS I: SHARING THE GOOD THINGS
1. C.S. Lewis, *Mere Christianity* (London: Fontana Books, 1970), 77–78.
2. Ronald J. Sider, "A Modest Proposal for Christian Giving in a Starving World: The Graduated Tithe," *Theology, News and Notes*, October 1975, 15.
3. John Wesley, *Works*. Cited by Kemper Fullerton, "Calvinism and Capitalism," in *Protestantism and Capitalism: The Weber Thesis and Its Critics*, ed. Robert W. Green (Boston: D.C. Heath, 1959).

CHAPTER 7: BASIC NEEDS II: FOOD AND CLOTHING
1. Doriz Janzen Longacre, *More-With-Less Cookbook* (Scottdale: Herald Press, 1976), 14.
2. Roland L. Weinsier, Sarah L. Morgan, and Virginia Gilbert Perrin, *Fundamentals of Clinical Nutrition* (St. Louis: Mosby, 1993), 7.
3. Weinsier et al., 4–5.
4. Longacre, 13.
5. Christie Harris and Moira Johnston, *Fig-Leafing through History* (New York: Atheneum, 1971).

CHAPTER 8: BASIC NEEDS III: A PLACE TO GO AND A WAY TO GET THERE
1. "Inside Out," *The Edmonton Journal*, 19 February 1994, E-1.
2. Ibid.

CHAPTER 9: THE OTHER NEEDS
1. A.W. Tozer, *I Talk Back to the Devil* (Harrisburg: Christian Publications, 1972), 29.
2. A.W. Tozer, *The Root of the Righteous* (Harrisburg: Christian Publications, 1955), 25.
3. Charles H. Spurgeon, *Faith's Checkbook* (Chicago: Moody, n.d.), 160.

CHAPTER 10: PUTTING THINGS IN PLACE
1. Martin Goldfarb, "Canada's Credo: Honesty Pays," *Reader's Digest,* June 1971, 30.
For a different approach to the validity of official measurements of poverty, see
Chilman, Cox and Nunnally, 107–108.
2. C.S. Lewis, *The Screwtape Letters* (London: Fontana Books, 1970), 109.
3. A.W. Tozer, *The Pursuit of God* (Harrisburg: Christian Publications, 1948), 21ff.
4. F. Green, "My Goal Is God," *Hymns of the Christian Life* (Harrisburg: Christian
Publications, 1936), 351.

CHAPTER 11: WHERE WE ARE, AND WHERE WE'RE GOING
1. Robert W. Green, *Protestantism and Capitalism: The Weber Thesis and Its Critics*
(Boston: D.C. Heath, 1959), vii.
2. R.H. Tawney, *Religion and the Rise of Capitalism,* New American Library (New
York: Mentor Books, 1954), 206.
3. Marquis W. Childs and Douglass Cater, *Ethics in a Business Society,* New American
Library (New York: Mentor Books, 1954), 55.
4. From John Wesley, *Works.* Cited by J.H. Plumb, *England in the Eighteenth Century,*
Pelican History of England, vol. 7 (London: Penguin Books, 1963), 97.
5. Aleksandr I. Solzhenitsyn, *The Gulag Archipelago* (New York: Harper & Row, 1974), 591.
6. "The Prospects for Humanity." Interview with Arnold J. Toynbee, Canadian Broad-
casting Corporation, October 27, 1975.

Printed in the United States
118205LV00002B/95/A

9 781573 831383

FOR KIDS
WHO LOVE ANIMALS
A Guide to Sharing the Planet

by
LINDA KOEBNER

illustrated by
THOMAS C. WHITTEMORE

edited by
**STEPHEN ZAWISTOWSKI, Ph.D., and
MICHAEL KAUFMANN**
for
**The American Society for the
Prevention of Cruelty to Animals**

LIVING PLANET

P R E S S

Los Angeles

For my son, Ian, whom I love more than any other animal in the whole wide world.

— L. K.

Published in the United States by Living Planet Press,
558 Rose Avenue, Venice, California 90291

Distributed by Publishers Group West, Emeryville, California

Activities created by: Helena Zengara
Interior design and page layout: Karen Bowers
Cover design: William Whitehead and Annmarie Dalton
Printing and binding: The Banta Company

ISBN: 1-879326-03-5

Discounts for bulk orders are available from the publisher.
Call (213) 396-0188.

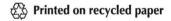 **Printed on recycled paper**

Manufactured in the United States of America

Library of Congress catalog card number 90-064450

10 9 8 7 6 5 4 3 2 1

CONTENTS

AUTHOR'S ACKNOWLEDGMENTS

First, thank you Lorraine Slater. And thanks always to my mother and Hans, who let me be a kid who loves animals. Special thanks to Helena Zengara, who designed the activities for this book. From her first words to me at the zoo, Helena has been a wonderful friend and a great educator. Special thanks also to my good friend Thomas C. Whittemore, who drew all the marvelous illustrations on these pages. I also want to extend my appreciation to Patti Forkan who, through her dedication and focus, has worked to make real changes in the way animals are treated; to Sam and Minna Edelman, who gave me a home where I could share my love of animals; and always to Jane Goodall.

Thanks especially to Stephen Zawistowski and Michael Kaufmann of the Humane Education Department at the ASPCA who invited me in, shared tofu soup, good stories, and great ideas; and to John Kullberg, president of the ASPCA, for putting the resources of America's oldest humane society behind this project. Thanks also to Joshua Horwitz and Dinah Berland at Living Planet Press, who saw the need for this book and made it happen.

And a note of thanks to all the kids who read the manuscript first: Olivia Billet, Constantino Gutierrez, Ian Koebner, Memy Melnick, Aran Nulty, Justine Schwartz, Josh and Anna Daisy Viertel, and Matthew Zawistowski.

Thank you, Ron, for always being there. And my thanks and deepest love to my dog, Taysa—my friend, my protector, and my companion for sixteen years. Thanks, too, to all the other animals in my house who kept me company as I wrote this book.

JUST FOR KIDS

This book is just for you—because you care about animals, and because you are a wonderful kind of animal yourself! This book will tell you astounding facts about all kinds of animals—like the one that may be curled up on your sofa and others in far-off lands. It will also tell you how some animals are in trouble and what you can do to help. I hope it will help you make decisions for yourself about how you can share the Earth with other animals.

Since this is your book, you can read it any way you want—back to front, front to back, or skipping between chapters. To make it even more fun, get a notebook and label it your "Animal Protection Notebook." Then, every time you see the picture on the right, take out your special notebook and get ready to write. For some activities at the end of each chapter—especially the messy ones—you may need an adult's supervision. Also,  be on the lookout for WILD WORDS in each chapter. You can find out what they mean in the Glossary at the end of the book.

I wish I'd had a book like this to help me understand animals when I was a child. I've loved animals all my life. When I was a baby, sometimes there were four or five cats in my crib at once. When I was in high school, I got to know a chimp who was learning how to communicate with sign language. I also studied monkeys and apes. And I met Jane Goodall, the famous scientist who studies chimpanzees. She wrote the Preface to this book because she knows how important it is for children to care.

Even if you don't grow up to be a scientist who studies animals, animals will always be part of your world. And you can help them, too. So why not start right now?

—*Linda Koebner*

TO PARENTS, TEACHERS, AND FRIENDS

With so much of the natural world at stake, helping children develop a reverence for life is vital. In fact, providing them with a humane education may be one of the most important things we ever do.

Loving animals comes naturally to kids. But we must teach them how to respect the fellow creatures on our planet, set good examples of empathy toward animals, and demonstrate our concern about the environment as a whole. If we don't, we may leave our children and grandchildren with a greatly impoverished natural world to enjoy as adults.

This book can help. It encourages awareness with lots of easy, fun activities. It also provides profiles of caring individuals—scientists, educators, and authors—who can serve as models for positive change.

Humane education can do many things. It can serve as an antidote to images of cruelty and violence in the media. And it can help children develop an appreciation for the rights of fellow humans as well as nonhuman animals.

Some of the ideas and activities in this book may challenge you and your own view of the world. By engaging in conversation with your children, grandchildren, and students about the way we live with the animals in our lives and wild creatures everywhere, you may find yourself asking why things are the way they are. If you also start to wonder how we can work together to make our world a safer place for all creatures, we all stand to benefit.

—*Stephen Zawistowski, Ph.D.*
Vice President for Humane Education
The American Society for the Prevention of Cruelty to Animals (ASPCA)

PREFACE

When I was a child I spent hours and hours watching the insects and birds and squirrels who lived in our backyard. I went on "nature walks" watching and writing down what I saw. And I read books and more books to learn about animals living in other parts of the world, especially Africa. I began to dream of the day when I could go there myself and study animals in the wild. Most people thought I was crazy. In those days girls didn't do things like that. But my mother always said, "Jane, if you want to do something enough, and you work very hard, you'll manage somehow." And so eventually, I saved up enough money to sail to Africa. My dream came true. And this year I am celebrating the thirtieth anniversary of the day I first began to study our closest living relatives, the chimpanzees.

It is wonderful to sit quietly in the forest among a couple of wild chimpanzees, to know that they trust you. If only everyone could share that experience. Chimpanzees are so like us. In the wild, the youngsters play together, much as you do. They run to their mothers if they are hurt. They

watch what adults do and imitate their behavior. And so they learn the right way to behave. Often their mothers punish them if they are disobedient.

Chimpanzees teach us that we are not as different from other animals as people used to think. Not only chimpanzees but other animals—like cats and dogs and elephants and dolphins and eagles and many more—have feelings like happiness and sadness and fear and despair. They can feel pain. They have minds that can help them solve the problems they come up against. And each one has his or her own personality, just as we do. If only everyone realized all this, then people would have more respect for animals and understand how arrogant we humans are, believing that we have the right to treat animals the way we like. Sadly, we are always doing bad things to animals.

For one thing, humans are destroying the wild places where animals live, cutting down the forests, building roads and shopping malls and parking lots. Humans are polluting the air and water and poisoning the animals and plants with pesticides. Wild animals are hunted, not only by people who need the meat to live, as in many parts of Africa, but also for "sport" by people who actually enjoy killing magnificent living beings. Animals are trapped and skinned so that people can wear their fur.

A lot of people seem to think that animals are only here to be our slaves. Many animals, even chimpanzees, are used for learning about human diseases. Many more are used to test the safety of products like cosmetics and shampoo. Chickens and cows and pigs are kept in horribly overcrowded, dirty, smelly cages and pens on "factory farms" and never know a moment's freedom in their lives. Puppies are often raised in miserable conditions. Unwanted kittens are thrown out like garbage. Dogs and cats are often abandoned when their owners move, and left to find food if they can. Many kinds of animals are made to perform in circus acts or commercials. I could list many other ways in which we are cruel to animals.

Probably you think that all this is terrible, but that you are too young to do anything about it. That's not true. The trouble is, it's not always easy to say what you think, especially if an adult or a bigger kid is doing something you think is wrong. But if you don't try to do something, you may always regret it. I still feel angry at myself because when I was a little girl, fifty years ago, I once saw some big boys pulling the legs off a crab and I didn't try to stop them. Animals can't speak for themselves—they need us to speak for them.

There is so much wrong with the world that many people feel helpless. What can one person do, after all? A lot. For there are many problems, close to home, that we *can* do something about. And this book will tell you how.

One thing I believe, when it comes to sharing our beautiful planet with animals, is this: Only when we understand can we care. Only when we care will we help. Only if we help shall they be saved.

For Kids Who Love Animals is your personal invitation to understand, to care about, and to help save animals.

Jane Goodall

1 WHAT KIND OF ANIMAL ARE YOU?

Some are bigger than a city block, and others smaller than your teeth. Some change skins. Others change identities, like Superman in his phone booth. Big, small, fat, tall, squishy, or hard—they are covered in skin, scales, hair, wool, or feathers. They leap, swim, burrow, hover in the air, or run as fast as a car. They are funny, cute, weird, scary, and sad. In some places, there are so many of them, they can be a nuisance. In other places, so few of them are left, they could disappear from the world forever. They come in so many shapes, sizes, and colors, their variety is amazing. What are they? Animals, of course!

? CAN YOU GUESS
. . . .

Which one has more bones in its neck—a mouse, a human, or a giraffe?

(Answer: Each one has seven neck bones.)

"What kind of animal are you?"

DID YOU KNOW?

Millions of animal "species" live on the Earth, fly above it, and swim in its rivers and seas. That includes us human animals. That's right, people are animals, too! Our species is called *Homo sapiens*—human beings.

No matter how different we look or how differently we behave, all of planet Earth's animals have certain things in common. We live, we grow, and we reproduce. And each kind of animal plays a part in making the world what it is.

All animals have certain basic needs. They must have air to breathe, food to eat, water to drink, and a home or shelter for protection. To live happy lives, most animals must also have companionship. And to reproduce, most of them need mates. One of the most important ways that animals are different from nonliving things—like rocks, chairs, or TV sets—is that animals sense things. They can see, smell, hear, taste, and touch. In fact, some animals can do some of these things even better than we can! Animals are aware of the world around them. And they have feelings, too.

By looking at fossils, scientists have figured out that animal life first began in the ocean. Over millions of years, animals have evolved, changing in many ways. Some crawled up on the land to live, some learned to fly, and some went back to live in the water. Each kind of animal has adapted to its environment in its own way.

Some animals have scales, some have feathers, and some have fur. Some live on land and some live in the water. Some fly, some walk, and some crawl. Some give birth to their babies and some lay eggs. Each species is unique. It not only looks, acts, and reproduces in its own way, it also needs different kinds of food and shelter and even has different ways of breathing.

Every animal species is part of a larger group. Here are the six groups you probably know best and what makes each one so special.

Insects
If one of every kind of animal in the world were invited to a football game, almost the whole stadium—about 83

"I think the insects are ahead!"

percent of it—would be filled up with insects. Human beings would fill only a few seats. There are more than a million different kinds of insects in the world, and they live just about everywhere. An insect has six legs, three sections to its body (thorax, abdomen, and head), and an "exoskeleton" (a skeleton on the outside of its body—like a hard jacket).

Fish

Fish were the first animals to develop backbones. Animals with backbones are called "vertebrates." (Animals without backbones are called "invertebrates.") Fish have gills for breathing in the water and are cold-blooded, which means their body temperatures adjust to the temperature of the air or water around them. Although most fish live in oceans, lakes, rivers, or streams, some fish can walk on land

INSECTS ARE EVERYWHERE
How many kinds of insects can you name? Where does each one live? Draw a picture of an insect. Count its legs. Does it have six? Count its sections. Does it have three?

(walking catfish) and some live in small pools of water in the desert (Gobi fish). Scientists have identified about 30,000 species of fish in all.

Amphibians

Have you ever seen tadpoles in a stream? If you could visit the stream every day for a few weeks, you might see the tadpoles turning into frogs. Amphibians—including frogs, toads, newts, and salamanders—are vertebrates that go through "metamorphosis." This means that they completely change as they grow to be adults. In fact, baby amphibians don't look like their parents at all. Tadpoles hatch from frog eggs and have tails. They swim around in the water just like fish. But as the tadpole grows, its tail disappears, legs grow on its body, and it develops lungs for breathing air. And then it isn't called a tadpole anymore— it's called a frog. The frog can use its legs to jump right out of the water and onto the shore or a log, if it wants to. There are about 2,500 different kinds of amphibians on Earth, and all of them transform as they grow.

Reptiles

About 6,000 species of reptiles live on Earth today. They are cold-blooded vertebrates, like fish and amphibians. Reptiles have scales and most of them lay leathery eggs. The most famous reptiles are the dinosaurs, which mysteriously disappeared from Earth millions of years ago. Did you know that some dinosaurs lived in the ocean and others flew through the air? Even though dinosaurs are extinct, many reptiles today look a lot like them. One of these is the rare Komodo Dragon, which can grow to be 10 feet long and weigh as much as 350 pounds.

Birds

A bird is a warm-blooded animal with feathers, hollow bones, a bill, and a muscular breastbone to help flap its wings. Birds lay hard-shelled eggs. There are 8,600 different species of birds. Some, like the hummingbird, are very small. Others, like the ostrich, are so big and strong they can protect themselves from predators just by kicking. Some birds sing and others, like parrots and mynah birds, have voices that sound like human speech. Many birds migrate, flying thousands of miles to build their nests and then flying back again.

Mammals

What kind of animal are you? A mammal, of course! The big family of mammals includes dogs, cats, gerbils, monkeys, cows, horses, pigs, zebras, and 4,245 other mammal species. All mammals are warm-blooded. That means their bodies stay the same temperature all the time. A mammal also has a backbone and hair (or fur) and gives birth to young that look just like their parents, only smaller. How do you suppose mammals got their name?—from their mothers. Female mammals nurse their babies with milk from their "mammary glands."

"I don't remember seeing anything this big at the zoo!"

MAMMAL NAMES
How many mammals can you name? Write their
names or draw their pictures in your "Animal
Protection Notebook."

Amazing mammals

In some parts of the world, very unusual kinds of
mammals have appeared. Even though they are mammals,
"monotremes"—including the platypus and echidna—lay
eggs. And "marsupials"—such as kangaroos, koalas,
wombats—have pouches
where their babies grow after
they are born.

And even though
they live in the water,
whales and dolphins are
mammals, too. They
breathe air and give birth
to their babies in the
water. The blue whale is
not only a big mammal, it
is the biggest animal in the
world. It can grow to be
100 feet long and weigh up
to 300,000 pounds. And
which kind of animal could

celebrate the most birthdays (if it could celebrate at all)? The tortoise takes the cake! Some tortoises have lived to be as old as 150!

For a very long time, humans believed they were the only ones with the ability to communicate. But now we know that many animals have their own ways of talking. For people, that means having words to say. For other animals, such as whales and dolphins, "songs" tell the story. Elephants rumble, bees dance, and many other animals signal each other, too. By watching chimpanzees, we have learned that other animals besides humans can use tools, too. Chimps make probes from sticks to get termites out of their mounds. And they really love to eat termites!

A CROWD OF HUMANS

Animals in groups are called all sorts of things. You've probably heard of "a school of fish." Below are a few more names of animals and animal groups. In your notebook, number your page from 1 to 5. Copy each phrase and complete it with the name of the animal group you think is right. (Answers are upside-down below.)

1. a _____ of rhinoceroses	troop
2. a _____ of whales	knot
3. a _____ of geese	gaggle
4. a _____ of monkeys	crash
5. a _____ of toads	pod

(1. crash 2. pod 3. gaggle 4. troop 5. knot)

ANIMALS IN TROUBLE

Animals get into trouble or are hurt for many reasons. As you will find out in this book, many of the world's animals are being destroyed by the actions of human beings. Here are the most common reasons that animals are in trouble today:

Habitat destruction. People are destroying the homes of

many wild animals. (We'll tell you more about "habitats" in Chapter 2.)

Pollution. As people pollute the world, they are damaging the planet and the animals that live on it.

Hunting. Animals are hunted and killed for food, for fur, or just for sport.

Ignorance. Some animals get a bad reputation from myths or stories that are not true. Have you ever heard of the "Big Bad Wolf"? Here are some other untrue things people have said about animals:

- Bats get caught in your hair.
- Snakes are slimy.
- Toads cause warts.
- Black cats are bad luck.

Sometimes, people just don't like certain animals and try to kill them. Some people don't believe that animals can feel pain. They don't think animals deserve to be treated with care and respect. That's when animals get into the biggest trouble.

Animals have rights

Every state has laws that protect the rights of animals, including:

- Protection from cruel treatment
- Protection from abandonment
- Protection from poisoning
- Provision for food, water, and shelter

Even though there are laws to protect animals, these laws are not always enforced. It is up to each of us to be aware of what can happen to animals and how we can help protect them. As you read this book, you will learn many ways to care for animals, even animals you'll never see. When you care for animals, you make the world a better place for them and for you.

PROTECTOR PROFILE
. . . .

THE STORY OF HENRY BERGH (1818–1888)

Henry Bergh was the founder of The American Society for the Prevention of Cruelty to Animals (ASPCA). He fought for laws to protect animals and children.

"Stop it, stop beating that horse at once!! Stop it I say!" The thin, tired horse had fallen to the pavement, unable to pull the heavy wagon one more foot. But his owner continued to whip him and scream for him to get up. A gentleman named Henry Bergh raced over and grabbed the whip

Henry Bergh hated to see that horse being beaten! So he did something about it.

away from the startled wagon driver. Beginning with that single, brave act of protecting a horse from its cruel owner, Bergh took the first important step toward changing the way animals could be treated in the United States.

A very wealthy man, Bergh was born in 1818 and grew up in New York City. When he stopped to help the carriage horse, he was living in Russia, where he had been sent by President Abraham Lincoln to be a diplomat. When Bergh returned to America, he knew what he had to do. Following the example of The Royal Society for the Protection of Animals in Great Britain, Bergh started The American Society for the Prevention of Cruelty to Animals (ASPCA), the first humane society in the United States, which officially opened in 1866.

Next, he worked on getting laws passed. Some of the early laws gave rights to horses, and protected cattle and other animals. The ASPCA was given the authority to enforce these laws. This was very important, because if the people who abused animals were not caught and punished, the laws meant nothing.

Even though some people thought they were crazy to make such a fuss about animals, Bergh and his colleagues believed in what they were doing. They continued working to protect animals, and many other cities soon started organizations to do the same. Laws to protect animals even led to laws that protect children. The Society for Prevention of Cruelty to Children (SPCC), the first society for the prevention of cruelty to children, was made possible because of the ASPCA.

Henry Bergh took action when he saw something he felt was wrong and cruel. Thanks to his work, millions of people have become aware of why hurting an animal is wrong, and a great difference has taken place in the way animals have been treated in this country for the past 125 years.

WHAT YOU CAN DO

Here are some of the things you can do to protect animals:

❑ Add the telephone numbers of your local veterinarian and your neighborhood animal shelter to the list of emergency numbers in your home.

❑ If you see someone hurting an animal—or if you see a stray dog or cat or an injured animal—ask an adult to help you contact the local animal shelter or humane society.

❑ Start an "Animal Protection Club" at your school, in your neighborhood, or at your church or temple. Club members can be on the lookout for stray cats and dogs and injured wildlife. You can also invite people from the humane society or animal shelter to come to your club and tell you how you can do more to help the animals in your area.

WILD WORDS

- Cold-blooded
- Environment
- Exoskeleton
- Invertebrate
- Mammary gland
- Marsupial
- Monotreme
- Species
- Thorax
- Vertebrate
- Warm-blooded

❏ Never leave trash lying around on the ground in parks or picnic grounds, and snip apart plastic six-pack holders before you throw them away. Ducks and other animals often get their necks caught in these plastic rings. Also, make sure not to throw away sharp objects like razor blades or cans with sharp edges without wrapping them up first.

❏ Join with your friends or school group to clean up a beach, park, or river bank.

What's wrong with this picture?

(Answer: broken bottle, six-pack rings, sharp can. Trash like this could hurt the ducks.)

ACTIVITY: MAKE YOUR OWN FOSSIL

Finding a real fossil is terrific! Fossils are rocks that contain the imprint of bones, shells, or leaves that existed thousands—maybe even millions—of years ago. You may not find a real fossil very often—or ever. But you can make your own fossil. Read these directions first, then try it.

You will need:
- 1 small bag of plaster of Paris (ask at a hardware store)
- Water
- 1 empty coffee can
- 1 old aluminum pie or cake pan
- Something to stir with (like a paint-stirring stick)
- Some small objects to press into your fossil (shells, leaves, stones, buttons, bottle caps, even your hand will do)
- A piece of picture-hanging wire (if you want to hang your fossil on the wall)
- A cup

How to do it:
1. Spread newspapers on the floor or table where you are going to work. (This can get messy!)
2. Collect your "fossil objects."
3. Pour a cup of plaster of Paris into the coffee can.
4. Stir in enough water until it looks like thick pancake batter, following the directions on the box.
5. Pour the plaster of Paris mixture into the aluminum pan.
6. Place your fossil objects on the plaster and press down firmly.
7. If you want to hang your fossil on the wall when it's dry, twist a piece of wire into a loop and stick it into the top of the mold.

8. Wait 5 minutes, then carefully remove the objects.

9. Let the plaster dry, remove it from the pan, and YOU HAVE MADE A FOSSIL!!

If you can't get plaster of Paris, you can also make a fossil with clay.

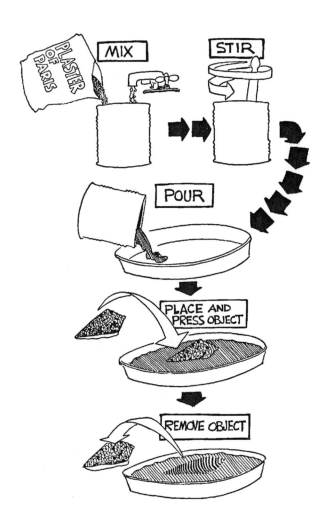

2 HABITAT IS WHERE IT'S AT

What do you suppose a pond, an ice floe, your kitchen drawer, a telephone pole, and the sands of the Mojave Desert all have in common? They are homes to animals. An animal's home is called its "habitat." This is where an animal finds everything it needs to survive—food, water, and shelter. An animal's habitat is also where it finds its mate, has babies, and finds protection from other animals. What's your habitat—a big city, a suburb, a small town, a farm? Some animals, like whales, need a habitat as big as an ocean. Others, like fleas, don't need much space at all, just a spot on a dog's back.

"Wow—there's just the habitat we've been looking for!"

CAN YOU GUESS

What is the coldest place in the world where animals live? What is the hottest?

(Answer: Antarctica, where penguins live, has recorded temperatures of minus-96 degrees F. In Death Valley—where jack rabbits, snakes, and lizards live—temperatures can rise as high as 134 degrees F.)

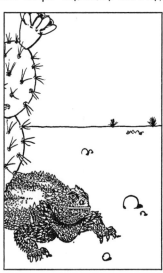

Some penguins live in the cold.

Horned toads like it hot.

DID YOU KNOW?

Over millions of years of evolution, animals have adapted to different places in different ways. Amazingly, different kinds of animals all manage to get the food they need, find mates, and defend themselves, wherever they might live.

If you lived in the Sahara Desert, you would need very different kinds of clothes than if you lived at the North Pole. Animals can't change clothes, so their bodies need to be naturally suited to the places in which they live. In hot, dry climates, like a desert, an animal needs to keep as much moisture in its body as possible, because it has very little water to drink. The camel is terrific at this. It can travel for days through the heat of the desert without drinking. Animals that live in cold climates need to stay warm in freezing temperatures, so they have their own "fur coats." Polar bears and walruses also have lots of fat—called "blubber"—beneath their fur to keep them warm.

Some animals have very unusual homes—such as hermit crabs, which live in the shells left behind by sea snails. Medusa fish live under the protective tentacles of the poisonous Portuguese man-of-war. Some African termites live in mounds of dirt 20 feet high.

Animal travelers

If you live in the north, where the winters are cold, maybe you like to visit your friends or relatives in the south during your winter vacation. Some animals like to travel, too, but they do it for survival, not just for fun. They move from one habitat to another in search of food. This is called "migration."

Have you ever seen geese flying south when the weather begins to get cold? Do they rest in parks or ponds near your home? Geese live in the north, then migrate south in winter when the days get shorter and snow covers the plants they eat. When the days get longer in spring and the weather warms up again, the geese fly back north to build their nests.

Did you know that southern hemisphere birds migrate from south to north for the winter? One bird, called the Wilson's storm petrel, flies all the way from Antarctica to California in the fall and back again in the spring—a round trip of 22,000 miles. That's a big winter vacation! Many

WILD NEIGHBORS
What kind of wild animals live in your neighborhood?
Do you see these animals in the spring, in the fall, or
all year round? Do they migrate? How do these
animals find shelter, what do they eat, and where do
they have their babies?

other animals migrate, too: whales, monarch butterflies, salmon, eels, and "nomadic" tribes of people travel long distances each year to find food.

ANIMALS IN TROUBLE

What would it be like to come home one day and discover that your house or apartment building were no longer there—that it had been destroyed, crunched up? Not only that, but what if you had no way to get food or water, and the road were cut off, so you could not even reach your friend's house? This is what we do to animals every time we cut down forests, pave a highway, or pollute the ocean.

People are just learning about how important it is to share the planet with animals, and we need to learn a lot more. Habitat destruction means that animals that once lived in a certain place are now homeless. Sometimes people destroy a path of migration and migrating animals are

One tree can be a home to many different creatures. How many animal homes can you find in this picture? What do you think would happen to these animals if just one tree were cut down? What would happen if the whole forest habitat were cleared away?

trapped without food or far away from the place they usually go to build their nests, lay their eggs, or give birth to their young.

Habitats can be changed by nature as well as by people. Natural changes, such as hurricanes, forest fires, and floods, all cause serious damage to animal homes and habitats. But unlike changes caused by humans, these natural changes usually lead to different kinds of habitat where other animals can live. A big forest fire, for example, may burn all the trees, but then new plants will grow on the forest floor, which makes food for other animals.

But when people cut down trees and destroy the forests, the chance for animals to find a natural home there is lost. The rainforests of South America are being cut down at a rate of 50 acres a minute. As you read this book, the homes of many monkeys, iguanas, snakes, butterflies, about 2,600 species of birds, and even more kinds of beautiful flowers and trees are being destroyed.

People also pollute bays and rivers, spill oil in the ocean, and make garbage that ends up in landfills or the ocean. These all destroy animal habitats.

Peregrine falcons used to live on cliffs overlooking lakes and ponds. Because much of their habitat has changed, some have adapted and now live on high buildings in the city. But not all animals are as adaptable as the peregrine falcon. The ancient forests of the Pacific Northwest are being cut down for wood. If these forests disappear, many birds and other animals will disappear, too.

All animals, including humans, need habitats. If we learn to share the planet with animals, instead of destroying their habitats, all the creatures of the Earth will have a better chance at survival. (In the next chapter, you'll find out more about the web of life that connects us all.)

What's wrong with this picture? What would be a better habitat for each animal?

PROTECTOR PROFILE
....

JACQUES-YVES COUSTEAU (1910–)

Can you imagine what it must have been like for explorers such as Marco Polo, Christopher Columbus, and all the other brave people who set out on an ocean voyage centuries ago? From the decks of their little ships, they could see nothing but water. Perhaps they would see sea turtles and pods of whales swim by and dolphins leap out of the waves. They must have wondered what went on under

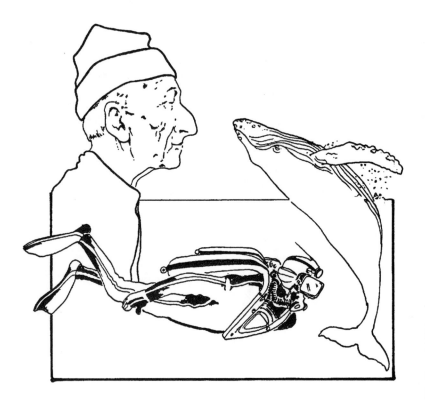

the sea, how deep the water was, and what secrets of underwater life were hidden from human eyes.

The mystery of habitats beneath the sea still has not been fully explored. But, one man has done a great deal to give us a peek at the world under the ocean. Jacques-Yves Cousteau began his career in the French Naval Academy. While he was in the Navy, he began his diving experiments and, in 1943, he and Emile Gagnan designed and built the Aqua Lung. This device allowed people to dive below the surface and explore the ocean without a submarine or tether.

From then on, Captain Cousteau worked to invent other ways for people to explore the world beneath the sea. He created the Diving Saucer and found ways for humans to live underwater for as long as three weeks. To document life under the sea, he helped invent cameras that would work underwater. In 1950, he bought an old naval ship called "Calypso," and turned it into a ship for oceanography.

As he explored the oceans, Cousteau became more aware of how marine life was suffering. Pollution, hunting, and fishing were disrupting this precious habitat. So he established The Cousteau Society to "increase awareness and knowledge of the beauty and fragility of our planet's resources." Captain Cousteau has produced more than a hundred films for television and three full-length films, as well as books and hundreds of articles to help bring the undersea world closer to those of us who cannot go there ourselves.

Jacques Cousteau received many awards for his work, but his greatest reward must have been that he helped people learn about the wondrous world of life under the sea. He helped people care about the animals whose homes are in the ocean and taught us how careful we must be to protect our underwater world.

WHAT YOU CAN DO

. . . .

We humans can hurt animal habitats, but we can help protect them, too. Here are some ways you can help:

❑ Clean up after picnics and remember to throw all your garbage away. (The average American creates more than 1,000 pounds of garbage every year.)

❑ Recycle your newspapers, aluminum cans, glass, and plastic. Remember that most garbage ends up in landfills or the ocean and can damage animal habitats.

❑ BEWARE OF PLASTIC! Sea mammals can swallow plastic bags, but they can't digest them, so this could cause the animals to die. Plastic garbage kills 2 million sea birds a year and hundreds of thousands of sea mammals.

❑ Be careful with balloons, and don't let them go, especially if you live near the ocean. When a balloon lands in the ocean, a sea turtle may think it's a jellyfish and try to eat it. This could kill the sea turtle.

WILD WORDS

- **Habitat**
- **Nomadic**
- **Migration**
- **Evolution**
- **Oceanography**
- **Rainforest**

HABITAT SWEET HABITAT

Some animals build or find special homes in their habitat. Write down the names of the animals below and which kind of home each one likes.

1.	beaver	lair
2.	bird	warren
3.	fox	lodge
4.	chipmunk	den
5.	rabbit	burrow
6.	wolf	nest

(Answer: 1. lodge 2. nest 3. lair 4. burrow 5. warren 6. den)

❏ Don't disturb an animal's nest.

❏ Be very careful to put out fires completely when you are camping or having a cookout. And never start a fire in places where fires are not permitted.

❏ Clean up your park. Join with your friends, school group, or club to clean up a habitat near your home.

❏ Plant a wildlife garden.

❏ Be thoughtful. Remember, if you litter or cause damage anywhere, you may be damaging an animal's home.

ACTIVITY: HOMES FOR SALE

Try this with a few friends or with a larger group. Write a classified ad for your favorite animal's home or habitat. Pick an animal, then read about it in books at home or in the library. Find out the following information:

- Where does the animal live?
- What kind of habitat does it live in (dry or wet, cold or warm)?
- Does it build a special type of home?
- What does it eat?
- What else does it need in its habitat?

After you have found out the answers, write a classified ad, just like the ones in your newspaper. The ad should describe a perfect home for the animal you have chosen. After you've written your ad, read it to your friends and see if they can guess what kind of animal it is. Here's an example:

> **AFRICAN GRASSLAND:** Prime savanna. Packed with antelope, gazelles, zebras, and other fantastic prey. Close to refreshing waterholes and shady acacia trees. Great for new pride just starting out. Call now. This habitat won't last!

What kind of animal would answer that ad? A LION, of course!

In a group, everyone can pick an animal, read about it, and write an ad. Then, each person takes a turn reading his or her ad and everyone else tries to guess the animal.

3 THE WEB OF LIFE

One beautiful spring day, a fluffy brown rabbit comes hopping out of its den after a long, snowy winter. Little does it know that a red-tailed hawk is flying high above, searching for food for its baby hawks back in the nest. The rabbit twitches its nose and settles down to eat the green grass that has just started to sprout. Suddenly, the hawk swoops down, grabs the rabbit, and carries it off to feed to its hungry baby birds.

This life-and-death scene is part of the "food chain"—the "who-eats-whom" of the animal world—and it happens every day in many ways. One animal that eats plants is eaten by another that eats animals. Animals that hunt other animals for food are called "predators." Those that are eaten are called "prey."

All animals get the energy they need to live and to grow either from eating plants or from eating other animals. Meat eaters are called "carnivores." Plant eaters are called "herbivores," and animals such as humans, who can eat both plants and animals, are called "omnivores."

Every community of plants and animals has many food chains. A community's animal and plant life and its food chains, together with the nonliving parts of that environment (climate, rainfall, mountains, houses) make up the "ecosystem." They are all connected. If we disturb any part of this connection, or web, we can disturb it all.

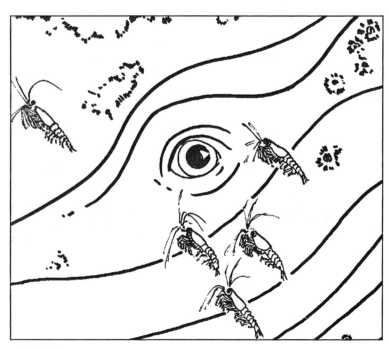

 CAN YOU GUESS

What do you think a big animal like a blue whale eats?

(Answer: The blue whale eats tiny shrimp, called krill—and lots of them. An average-sized whale can gobble up about 4-1/2 tons of plankton a day!)

DID YOU KNOW?

All living things are part of at least one food chain. Every animal and plant has a part to play. Animals compete with other animals to protect their homes, to get enough food, and to find a mate. But even though nature is full of conflict, it is also balanced, allowing a number of different species to survive.

Wolves, for example, are excellent predators. But they will usually choose the easiest animal to kill, like an old or sick deer that cannot keep up with the herd. And when wolves take the weakest of the herd for food, they leave the younger and stronger deer alive to breed. They also keep the herd from getting so big that there won't be enough grass for all the deer to eat.

FOOD CHAIN CLUES
Every animal has a place on the food chain. Find a squirrel, pigeon, rabbit, duck—or maybe an ant or a caterpillar—in your neighborhood, and watch it for a few minutes. What does it eat? Where does it find its food? Does it have predators? Where do you think it belongs on the food chain? If you don't know, read about that animal in the library and write down what you find out about it.

Animal pals

Animals cooperate with each other in many ways. The rhinoceros doesn't see very well. It is also bothered by ticks and other bugs that live on its hide. But the tick bird always comes to the rescue. The bird sits on the rhino and gobbles up the insects there. It also calls out a warning when it sees danger approaching. The tick bird gets a movable feast and the rhino gets a watchbird. This kind of cooperation between different species of animals is called "symbiosis."

Another little bird with an unusual job is the lapwing. It jumps into the crocodile's mouth and cleans the leeches and bits of food off the big reptile's teeth. The crocodile gets clean teeth and the bird gets a free lunch. And you can bet nobody will bother the lapwing when it's doing its job!

Some animals can cooperate, even though they've never met. What do you suppose an African bird called the honey guide likes? Honey, of course! And so does the badger. But the honey guide can find beehives that the badger can't— and the badger knows how to break the hives open. When a badger hears a honey guide singing and sees the bird circling in the air, it knows a beehive must be nearby. It follows the bird to the hive, breaks it open, and eats the honey. And there's always plenty of honey left for the badger's feathered friend.

Even animals and plants can be partners. The yucca plant and the yucca moth may seem an unlikely pair, but neither could survive without the other. The yucca plant's flowers are shaped so that no other insect or bird can help it reproduce. The yucca moth fits into the flower perfectly and helps the plant to "pollinate." This means it carries the flower pollen from plant to plant, helping more yucca plants to grow. In return, the moth has a safe place to lay its eggs and plenty of seeds for its moth larvae to eat.

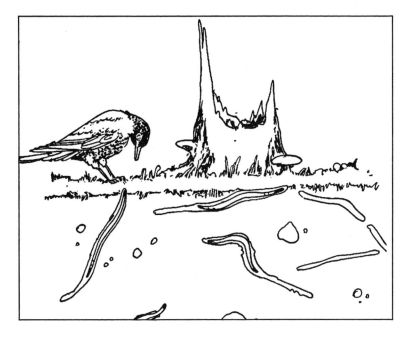

What do worms do all day?

Earthworms live all over the Earth and are busy eating dirt and turning it into topsoil all the time. According to Charles Darwin, the earthworms living in one acre of dirt can digest and eliminate 10 to 18 tons of topsoil a year. So, without worms, many plants would have no place to grow.

 **ANIMALS IN TROUBLE**

. . . .

Have you ever made a house of cards? It's not easy. Each card is balanced so carefully against another, you might even have to hold your breath to put the last card on top. All you have to do is touch it the wrong way, one card falls, and then—wham—the whole house collapses.

When the balance of nature is disturbed, something like

this can happen also. Sometimes the balance is disturbed because of a natural disaster—a fire or flood—but usually it's because humans have made a mess of the food web. In Chapter 2, you found out what can happen when an animal's habitat is destroyed. Here are some other ways that humans can disturb the balance of nature.

Pesticides

For a long time, people were pleased because they had found a new way to kill pests with chemicals. These chemicals, called "pesticides," are sprayed onto plants to kill the insects that eat them. But after a while, people noticed that insects were not the only creatures dying. Other wildlife was also being killed or poisoned.

The bald eagle almost became extinct because of what pesticides did to their eggs. Pesticides used on crops would wash into streams and lakes, and the fish who live there would absorb some. Bald eagles would catch and eat the fish. So the eagles got some pesticides in their bodies also. It wasn't enough to kill them, but it did make their eggshells so thin that when the eagles sat on the eggs, they cracked them, killing their own offspring. When people began to realize the damage pesticides were causing and stopped using them so much, the eagles started to produce healthy eggs again. But, it was almost too late.

The same kind of "chain reaction" happened in Borneo, where the dangerous pesticide DDT was used to kill houseflies. Reptiles, called geckos, ate lots of flies, which means they also ate lots of DDT. The cats ate many geckos, and they got so much DDT in their bodies that many cats died. With fewer cats as predators, the rats started taking over the area. Too many rats was a much worse problem than houseflies—so the humans of Borneo had to bring in more healthy cats to bring back the balance of nature.

"Oh, no, not those terrible tree eaters again! Where can we go now?"

Hunting animals to extinction

The dodo bird is famous because it no longer exists. This big bird, which lived on the little island of Mauritius, was hunted to extinction shortly after it was discovered, so people never had a chance to learn much about it. The dodo, which couldn't fly, was so slow that the sailors who came to the island called it a "stupid dodo." Because the sailors found it easy to kill for food, they helped themselves. Soon the sailors had killed so many dodos that the bird became extinct.

Shortly after the dodos were gone, people noticed that some special trees, called tambalocoque trees, were not growing. Some scientists think that the seeds from these trees sprouted only after passing through the bodies of the dodo birds, which ate the seeds for food. Goodbye dodos—goodbye tambalocoque trees.

Yesterday it was the dodo. Today it is the African elephant, the mountain gorilla, and many other animals threatened with extinction. And if animals become extinct before we can learn about them, we will never know the part they played in the food chain, or how important they might have been to the future of the planet.

PROTECTOR PROFILE
. . . .

RACHEL CARSON (1907–1964)

Imagine a lovely spring day in the country. The meadow is filled with colorful flowers, the trees are green, and the sky is bright blue. If you stop and listen, you can hear the songs of robins, cardinals, and sparrows. Listen more carefully, and you might hear the buzz of bees whizzing from flower to flower. At night, you fall asleep to the lullaby

Rachel Carson wanted to make sure that birds would always sing and there would never be a "silent spring."

of chirping crickets and croaking frogs.

Now, imagine a silent spring. No birds are singing, the bees don't buzz, and there's not a green tree or flower in sight. Rachel Carson imagined this. She spent her life studying biology and writing books and stories about nature. Her most famous book is called *Silent Spring*. She wrote it after a friend told her that DDT, a chemical used to kill insects, had also killed the birds around her home.

Rachel Carson began to study DDT and other chemicals and their effect on the environment. And what she found out was frightening. She learned that if the uncontrolled use of these chemicals continued, the animals, the plants, and the whole world of nature could be destroyed and someday there would be a silent spring.

When her book was published in 1962, it upset many people. Pesticides were used to protect plants from insects. How could enough food be grown if these chemicals were not used?

Soon however, people began to see the wisdom of Rachel Carson's words. The destruction of birds and bugs was a serious sign. It meant that the whole environment—the entire web of life, including humans—was in danger. The water, the soil, and the air on which life depends were all being poisoned by pesticides.

In a very real sense, Earth Day and the whole environmental movement were born when Rachel Carson imagined what a silent spring would be like and helped to prevent it. Working together, we can also help to make sure that spring days will always be filled with the sounds of life.

WHAT YOU CAN DO

❏ Instead of putting leaves in plastic garbage bags or burning them, try using them as mulch in your garden. Or take them to the woods. You will be providing nutrients for the soil and homes for insects.

❏ Instead of using insecticides to kill bugs, put up screens on your windows, make sure you don't leave crumbs around to attract ants or cockroaches, and cover your garbage.

❏ Don't disturb wildlife or plants. Leave nests where they are, and don't pull flowers out of the ground. Use your camera or make a drawing if you want to remember what natural things look like.

❏ Don't chase pigeons, ducks, or squirrels, and don't scare fish. Instead, find out where they belong on the food chain by watching them and reading about them.

WILD WORDS

- **Carnivore**
- **Ecosystem**
- **Extinction**
- **Food chain**
- **Herbivore**
- **Omnivore**
- **Pesticide**
- **Pollinate**
- **Predator**
- **Prey**
- **Symbiosis**

ACTIVITY: FOOD WEB MOBILE

Construct a mobile using your knowledge about food chains. A community or environment is made up of many different food chains. Many of the animals eat or are eaten by several different animals in the community. The mixing of these food chains makes up a food web. In a food chain there are lots of plants, fewer plant eaters (herbivores), and even fewer meat eaters (carnivores). So the shape of a food web comes out like a pyramid. The sun provides energy for life on Earth, helping the plants to grow and turn green. So the sun needs to be part of the food web, too.

You will need:
- Pictures of plants, herbivores, and carnivores
- Wire coat hanger
- String
- Scissors
- Glue or tape
- Construction paper
- Light wooden dowel or balsa wood

1. Decide on the animals and plants you want for your food chains and for your food web.

2. Place your first food chain in the center of the hanger. For example:

SUN
HAWK
RABBIT
GRASS

3. Slowly add plants, herbivores, and carnivores to opposite sides of the hanger to balance your mobile.

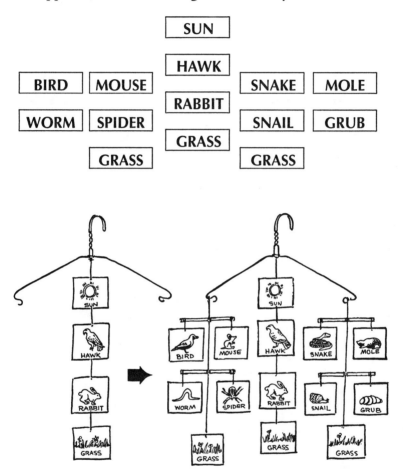

4. When your mobile is complete, hang it up. While you admire your work think about these questions: What would happen if one of the foods disappeared? If one of the animals became extinct? Would it put the mobile off balance?

4 FAVORITE ANIMAL FRIENDS

Perky, the fluffy green-eyed cat that lives with me, is sitting on my lap as I write this. She makes my job a little harder when she bumps my hand asking to be petted or tries to walk on the keyboard of my computer. But Perky's soft body, her gentle purr, and the way she looks up at me give me reasons to let her stay. In fact, I like having her with me very much.

Dogs and people are old friends.

CAN YOU GUESS

. . . .

How long have people and dogs been companions?

(Answer: Fossil evidence tells us that dogs and people have lived together for at least 10,000 years.)

DID YOU KNOW?

Some people call them "pets." Some people call them "companion animals." But whatever we call them, pets or companion animals, whether they are big or small, furred or feathered, they are often among our favorite friends. And if we take good care of them, they will be our friends for a very long time.

Having a companion animal is also a big responsibility. Your pet is not a toy that you can put away and forget about when you are bored with it. Your pet depends on you.

THE RIGHT PET FOR YOU

Just because you don't live in a house with a big yard doesn't mean you can't have a pet. But you want to make the right choice for yourself and your family, too. Remember, your companion animal will be a part of your family for a long time.

Before you decide which companion animal is the right one for you, ask yourself the following questions:

• Does everyone in your family agree to having a pet?

You may need help sometimes. Even if you are the one who will take care of the animal most of the time, you need everyone's support. What if you spend the night with a friend or get sick and can't feed your pet? Who will shop for your pet's food? Is anyone in your family allergic to cats or dogs?

• How much time can you spend with your pet?

What will happen if you are in school all day and then go to dance class? Will someone be at home to care for your companion? If you're away from home a lot, maybe a guinea pig, a bird, or a fish would be a better choice than a dog that wants your company.

• How much space do you have?

Do you live in an apartment in a big city or a house in the suburbs or a small town? Maybe you live in the country. Some pets don't need much space. Cats can be very happy in an apartment. So can birds, rodents, and fish. Dogs need more room to exercise. Imagine what it would be like to walk your dog several times a day—rain or shine, hot days or cold days—even when you don't feel like it.

• How much money can you spend on a pet?

Every companion animal needs food, regular care by a "veterinarian" (a doctor who takes care of animals), and supplies. And these things cost money. Some animals will be less expensive to take care of than others. A dog will cost more than a rabbit. Talk to your parents. Will the cost of care come from your allowance or other earnings? Will your parents pay for some of your pet's care?

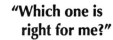

"Which one is right for me?"

• Do you already have other pets?

How will they adjust to a new animal in the house?

CHOOSING A COMPANION

The most common companion animals in America are cats and dogs. The most numerous are fish. But, lots of other animals make great companions, too. Here is a list of companion animals and information about what each kind must have besides food and medical care to stay healthy and happy. The codes show how much attention each animal needs, and how expensive it is to keep.

DOGS

Dogs are fabulous friends, and there are many different kinds from which to choose. A dog doesn't need to be a fancy breed to be a good friend. But it does need plenty of attention. You must have time to train your dog, time to play with it, and time to give it exercise. If you get a puppy, housebreaking your pet will take patience. But if you are ten years old now and you get a puppy, if all goes well the dog will be your companion until long after you graduate from high school. *** $$$

➡ **Must have:**

Training. Take the time to train your pet. The dog will be happier and so will you and everyone else. You don't want your dog to jump on people, run away, or chew the new couch.

Spaying or neutering. If a dog (or cat) is the pet for you, your companion should be spayed or neutered. This way it won't be able to have puppies (or kittens). It might seem like fun to let your pet have babies, but they are a lot of work. And there are never enough homes to go around.

ATTENTION :	*** High	** Medium	* Low
EXPENSE :	$$$ High	$$ Medium	$ Low

Besides, your pet will be healthier and better behaved if it is spayed or neutered.

CATS
Cats have wonderful personalities. They are affectionate and intelligent but much more independent than dogs. They need your company, but they can be left alone during the day as long as they have food, water, and a clean litter pan. If you live in an apartment building, make sure you have screens on the windows so your cat doesn't fall out. Of course, if you can have more than one cat, they can be great company for each other and lots of fun to watch. Cats are the most popular pets in the United States and if you get to know a cat you will see why. *** $$

➡ **Must have: Spaying** or **neutering** (see page 47).

RABBITS
Rabbits can be nice pets. They are cuddly and affectionate, and they can be housebroken. There are many different rabbits to choose from. There are little Dutch rabbits and huge Flemish giants. If you let them out of their cage in the house, keep an eye on them. Don't let them chew on electrical wires, which is a very dangerous habit they can have. (Do you suppose they think they're chewing on vines?) ** $

RODENTS
Hamsters, mice and rats, gerbils, and guinea pigs are all rodents that you can keep as pets. You don't need much space or much money to keep one of these cute companions in your home. You can choose males or females, but don't keep both together, or you might have unwanted litters.

➡ **Must haves (for all rodents):**
Give them **hard objects** to chew, such as pieces of wood

or bone, or else their teeth will get too long. Rodent teeth keep growing unless they gnaw on hard objects. Also give them a **salt lick.**

HAMSTERS. If you want a pet to care for but you don't have much space, a hamster may be the animal for you. You can watch as your little rodent builds a nest or stuffs its cheek pouches with seeds. Your hamster will happily explore the structures you make for it out of cardboard rolls and boxes. But it will probably redecorate the place. A hamster must be handled gently, so this may not be the right pet for a very young child. Hamsters are nocturnal animals. That means they sleep during the day and may keep you awake at night. * $

MICE and **RATS** (not always white, but bred as pets). These rodents are intelligent and gentle. They make great pets that are easy to care for. Some people are scared of rats or mice, but once you get to know them you will see how interesting they can be. * $

GERBILS. These desert rodents were only tamed as pets about 30 years ago. They have a lot of energy and need lots of exercise. They are more likely to be diurnal (awake during the day), so you can watch them play. * $

GUINEA PIGS. These rodents are wonderful pets. They are bigger than gerbils and hamsters and are easier to handle. Give them a clean, airy cage with a place to make a nest, and they will be happy. Guinea pigs will definitely get to know you and will whistle a welcome when they see you. Don't put them in a room with a TV set, though. The high frequency can hurt their ears. ** $

➡ **Must have:** Guinea-pig pellets containing **vitamin C,** which they need.

BIRDS

Birds don't need much besides fresh birdseed, water, gravel (to help them digest their food), and a cage to suit their habits. Birds are messy, though, and you will need to clean their cage about every week or so. Some birds like to take a bath. Get a birdbath to hang on the cage. But, when your birds are done flapping around in the water, make sure to dry their cage.

➡ **Must have:** Protection from drafts. Keep your bird out of drafty doorways and away from open windows.

CANARIES. These lovely yellow birds should be kept in pairs. Otherwise, they'll get lonely. The males sing, the females chirp. Also, they can be nervous, so move quietly and slowly around them. Cover the cage at night. * $

➡ **Must have:** A **big, wide cage** with enough room to fly and a **perch**.

PARAKEETS. These colorful, cheerful birds will give you lots of attention. As they get to know you, they can become very affectionate. But, if you are away from home a lot, consider getting two birds, because they get lonely by themselves. * $

➡ **Must have:** Parakeets like to climb up and down, so a **tall cage** and a **ladder** will make them happier.

FISH

You can't pet a fish or take it for a walk, but fish are beautiful and fun to watch. Although fish might seem easy to take care of, they need just the right conditions to live and stay healthy.

➡ **Must have:** Depending on the type of fish, they will need a fish bowl or **aquarium** which will have to be cleaned regularly. Put an **aerator** in the aquarium for oxygen and a **filter** to keep the water clean.

GOLDFISH. Goldfish are pretty hardy, but they do need the proper care. That means a big fish bowl or aquarium, plants, and enough freedom to swim. Don't crowd your fish. Remember each one-inch goldfish needs about one gallon of water. With the right care, goldfish will live long, grow big, and bring you pleasure for years. * $

TROPICAL FISH. Keeping an aquarium of tropical fish can be a great hobby. But it's not that easy. There are many varieties of tropical fish, often with different needs. Some fish are very expensive and some don't like each other. Do some research first. Talk to people who have raised tropical fish, and read books on how to take care of fish before you set up your aquarium. Make sure to get fish that have not been taken from the wild. If you can give these colorful animals the right conditions, you will learn a lot and have fun, too. ** $$
➡ **Must have:** An aquarium heater.

Where can you find a pet?

Once you decide what kind of pet you want, then you need to know where to find one. The first place to look for a dog or cat is at your local animal shelter. Shelters always have dogs and cats that really need a home and a friend. You might also find a rabbit, gerbil, or bird there.

If you want a special breed of dog or cat, ask your local shelter or humane society for the name of a responsible breeder. Then visit the breeder to see if the animals are being well cared for. Ask to see where the dogs live.

If you decide to go to a pet store instead, make sure that the store is clean and the animals are healthy.

ANIMALS IN TROUBLE

Every year 21 million cats and dogs are born in the United States. Every year 15 million end up in shelters or humane societies. Every year 10 million are "euthanized" (humanely killed) because there aren't enough homes for them. How can this happen to so many of our animal friends? Some people do not take responsibility for their animals. They get tired of their pets, or they move, or they realize proper care is expensive and a lot of work.

Abandoned animals

Some people just let their animals go or lock them out of the house to become strays. Stray animals get sick and go hungry. They are often hurt, and many die.

Overpopulation

To make matters worse, some people continue to let their dogs and cats have puppies and kittens even though they may not want them. Spaying and neutering are easy operations performed by a veterinarian to keep animals from having unwanted babies. Female dogs and cats are spayed. Males are neutered. Spaying or neutering also makes animals calmer and less likely to stray. If all pet owners would spay and neuter their pets, animal overpopulation would not continue.

Puppy mills

People love puppies. And pet shops know it. Many of the cute little puppies you see in some pet shop windows come from "puppy mills." These are places where females are kept in small, dirty cages and have one litter after the

HOW MANY KITTENS?
If, in two years, one male and one female cat have four litters of six kittens each and each of those kittens grows up and has three litters of five kittens each, and each of their kittens grows up and has two litters of five kittens each, how many kittens would be born in only two years?

(Answer: 3,600 kittens.)

next without proper medical care or nutrition. Dogs are very social animals. To be healthy and to like being with people, they need to be handled kindly from an early age. Nobody pets or cuddles puppies born in a puppy mill. They may be taken from their mothers before they are old enough and sent across the country to pet shops. So if you buy from a pet shop that gets its puppies from a puppy mill, you are likely to get an animal that is adorable on the outside, but filled with problems on the inside.

Wild animals

Wild animals are just that—wild. They are not tame, so they do not make good pets. Wild animals—such as turtles, monkeys, parrots, and snakes—belong in their natural habitat. Your home cannot meet their needs. And in many cases, keeping them as pets is against the law. Many animals have become endangered because so many have been taken from the wild.

PROTECTOR PROFILE

JAMES HERRIOT (1917–   )

Have you ever read *Moses the Kitten* or *Only One Woof?* These books were written by a veterinarian who has written many books about the animals he loves. As a country animal doctor in Yorkshire, England, James Herriot has spent most of his life caring for companion and farm animals. He has treated thousands of them, and still does.

The animal doctor and writer, whose real name is James A. Wright, grew up with his companion dog, Don. He was fascinated by dogs all his life and especially wanted to know

why these wonderful companion animals are so devoted to people, why they are so loyal and affectionate. He wanted to spend his life being with dogs, but he didn't know how.

Then the head of the Veterinary College of Glasgow, Scotland, came to his school. In 1930, there were few vets because not many people could afford to have companion animals. And most of the horses had been replaced by cars and trucks. But, James Herriot knew that this was the life for him. He pictured himself in a white coat, operating to save a dog's life. He worked very hard to become a vet. When he graduated, he found a job with an older veterinarian in the country. His partner loved horses and left the care of dogs to the young vet. Now, years later, Herriot writes stories about the dogs, cows, pigs, sheep, and goats he has come to know so well.

His life has not always been easy. A country vet gets up in the middle of the night to help a cow that is having a difficult birth, gets kicked into the mud by an angry horse, or drives for hours to care for a sickly puppy. He sees unhappiness and joy. James Herriot's true stories help us experience the fun, the companionship, and the devotion that humans and animals can share.

WILD WORDS

- Breed
- Companion animal
- Diurnal
- Euthanize
- Neuter
- Nocturnal
- Overpopulation
- Pet
- Puppy mill
- Spay
- Veterinarian

WHAT YOU CAN DO

❑ Be a responsible pet owner. Learn about how to take good care of your companion animal, and do it. Make sure your animal friend has:
  • Proper food and fresh water
  • Veterinary care
  • Exercise
  • Love

❑ Pet-proof your home. Like a human baby, animals can hurt themselves around electrical wires, hot stoves, or high places. Look for accidents before they happen.

❑ Never leave your dog closed up in a car, especially in the summer. The heat can quickly kill your dog, even with the windows partially open.

What's wrong with this picture?

❏ Make sure your dog has a license. This is for your pet's protection. If your dog does get lost, the license will help find him.

❏ Don't let your dog or cat run around without you. They may get lost, hurt, or stolen.

❏ Make sure you have your dog and cat spayed or neutered. Don't contribute to the pet overpopulation problem.

❏ Get your companion from an animal shelter. A "second-hand" dog can be a wonderful friend.

❏ Do not get a wild animal as a pet.

❏ If you do go to a pet store, ask the people there where they get their puppies and kittens. Buying a dog from some pet stores can encourage puppy mills to stay in business. Try to buy supplies from a store which does not sell dogs and cats.

❏ If you can't find the right dog at a shelter, ask the person in charge for the name of a responsible breeder.

❏ Report any stray animals you see to an animal shelter or the police.

❏ If for some reason you absolutely have to give up your companion, do not abandon it. Try to find a good home, or take it to an animal shelter. The animal may find a good home and a second chance.

ACTIVITY: PET CENSUS

Find out what types of companion animals other kids have and how they got their pets. Take a census either in your neighborhood or in your classroom. Ask if most of the pet owners have cats, dogs, parakeets, or some other type of pet (like rabbits, guinea pigs, gerbils, etc.). Find out if anyone has animals like snakes, parrots, or other wild animals which should not be pets.

Find at least five people to interview. Ask them the questions in the column on the left and write down their answers. In a larger group, ask the questions on the right and count how many people raise their hands.

Look at the answers people have given. Add up the numbers. How many people have how many pets? How many different kinds are there? Do more people have cats than dogs? Do most kids have a pet? Do any have wild animals as pets? Who takes care of them? Do they take their pets to the veterinarian?

After you know the answers, you can write a story for your school paper using the information you have gathered. You can also ask your teacher to invite a veterinarian or someone from your local animal shelter to come to your class-room and talk to your class about the proper care and treatment of pets.

Questions for one person	**Questions for a group** *(Raise hands to say yes.)*
★ What kind of pet do you have?	★ How many people have dogs? How many have cats?
★ Do you have more than one? How many?	★ Who has more than one?
★ What are they?	★ What are they?
★ Where did you get your pet—from a shelter, a pet store, a neighbor?	★ How many people got pets from a pet store?
★ Did you want your pet and choose it yourself, or did someone else choose it?	★ Did you choose it yourself? Did someone else choose it?
★ Was your pet a stray animal?	★ Was your pet a stray?
★ Who is responsible for the daily care of your pet?	★ Do you take care of your pet?
★ Do you take care of it or do your parents?	★ Do your parents take care of it?
★ Is your pet neutered or spayed?	★ Is it neutered or spayed?
★ Do you want your pet to have babies? Will you be able to take care of all of them?	★ If not, can you take care of lots of baby animals?
★ Has your pet been to a veterinarian for its vaccinations and checkup?	★ Have you taken your pet to a vet for shots and checkup?
★ Does your pet have an ID tag in case it gets lost?	★ How many people have IDs for their pets?

5 ANIMALS AT WORK

Jamie is a sixteen-year-old boy who has never seen a tree or another person. He has been blind since birth. All his life he has needed someone to help him go places. Now he is able to go wherever he wants and be independent. That's because his Seeing Eye dog, Prince, sees for him. Jamie can trust his safety completely to his new canine friend.

Other animals besides dogs are trustworthy helpers, too. In big cities, police officers often depend on horses. The officer and horse travel as a team through streets and parks, helping people in trouble and watching over large crowds.

Geese are good protectors, too. They don't like strangers to invade their territory. They honk loudly and run toward intruders, snapping their beaks to scare them away. Some people keep "guard geese" to protect their property in this way.

? CAN YOU GUESS
. . . .

How did people send airmail letters before there were airplanes?

(Answer: Homing pigeons could carry messages hundreds of miles through the air and back.)

DID YOU KNOW?
. . . .

Cats chase mice, dogs have a fabulous sense of smell, elephants can lift, pull, and shove heavy loads, and camels can walk for days in the desert. Using their natural abilities, animals help humans in many ways. For centuries, people have "domesticated" animals and put their natural talents to work. All over the globe, people have developed special partnerships with animals. Farmers, cowboys, policemen, bomb squads, soldiers, sailors, and explorers do their jobs better because animals help them.

Some animals can help people because they can do things that people can't. Camels can carry heavy loads and walk for days through the desert without water. Without them, transportation would be hard for people who live in the desert.

Good dogs

Over many centuries, the different breeds of dog we see today were bred to develop their natural abilities. That's why some breeds are so good at herding, others run fast, and some have such a good sense of smell that after an earthquake they can find people buried under collapsed buildings. Herding dogs are active and intelligent. And working dogs are usually larger and stronger.

My dog, Taysa, always runs between me and my son when we take a walk—back and forth, back and forth. It

These "ships of the desert" help people make long treks through the Middle East and Africa.

took me awhile to realize that she was still acting on her instinct to herd. Instead of sheep, she is working to keep her people together.

Royal cats

Cats were domesticated in ancient Egypt to keep rodents away from stores of grain. Amazed by the intelligence, beauty, and grace of cats, Egyptians worshipped them and treated them like kings and queens. One cat even had 2,000 servants! Egyptians also domesticated the pig, using it in the fields to dig up the earth with its snout and break clumps of dirt with its hooves as it walked along, making the fields easier to plant.

Humans have used the strength of animals for a long time. Before cars were invented, people used horses to pull their carriages and carts. Teams of horses and mules pulling covered wagons led the first American settlers out West. Before trucks and tanks came along, horses were also the brave transportation for warriors—carrying chiefs, kings, generals, and soldiers into battle.

Often when people cannot help other people, animals can. Handicapped children gain confidence by learning to ride on horses. The deaf can use specially trained dogs to listen for things they cannot hear. Elderly people often find love and laughter with companion dogs and cats. And these gentle animals also bring smiles to the faces of emotionally disturbed adults and children when no one else can.

ANIMALS IN TROUBLE

Unfortunately, people sometimes treat animal helpers badly. Remember Henry Bergh and the carriage horse that was being abused? Have you ever seen a dog tied up on a short chain without shelter from the sun, rain, or cold, guarding a gas station or factory? Or, if you live in a big city, you may see carriage horses pulling tourists through the busy traffic, breathing exhaust fumes next to honking cars and trucks.

Elephants will sometimes complain when they are forced to work too hard, trumpeting and throwing things around to tell people they don't like the way they're being treated. And some mules will stop in their tracks, refusing to budge. But other animals that are treated unfairly will just work until they're all worn out.

PROTECTOR PROFILE: JACK

The car pulls into a lot near the customs building at Kennedy Airport outside of New York City. The sun is barely up and there is a chill in the air. Still a bit groggy with sleep, Jack is glad when he and his human partner, Hal, enter the warm building to begin their day's work. They check in and walk quickly to the counter where they will inspect the baggage arriving from outside the country.

Jack loves his job. He has trained for many months. It is a very important job few can do. If he was not there to check baggage, then people might bring fruits, vegetables, and other plants into the country that are not allowed to be

WILD WORDS

- Canine
- Domesticate
- Homing pigeon
- Seeing Eye dog

here. These plants can be home to insects or bacteria that could quickly spread to the crops we eat. By keeping these items from entering the country, customs officials help prevent new diseases from spreading. Some of Jack's friends work in the customs department to locate drugs, but Jack works for the U.S. Department of Agriculture.

Jack and Hal go through hundreds of suitcases and packages during the morning. Finally, it is time for a break. Jack and his partner go outside for a quick walk and then sit down for a rest. Hal has a cup of coffee and Jack, the beagle, curls up for a well-deserved nap.

WHAT YOU CAN DO
. . . .

❑ Treat working animals with respect and care. If you see animals being misused, tell an adult, or let your local animal shelter know.

❑ Always ask permission of the owner before you go near a dog or touch it. This is especially important when you approach a Seeing Eye dog. Remember, the dog is responsible for the safety of its blind owner, and you might distract the dog from its work.

❑ If someone invites you to take a carriage ride in the city, say "No, thank you" if the horses are made to work on a hot day or if the streets are crowded with traffic.

What's wrong with this picture?

ACTIVITY: WORD SEARCH

Animals have helped people throughout history by providing us with food, shelter, clothing, and transportation. Animals have worked to carry loads, solve crimes, send messages, and assist us with everyday chores when we are unable to do things for ourselves.

DIRECTIONS:

Look for the names of working animals listed below that are hidden in the jumbled letters on the left. (Remember: words can be spelled backward, horizontally, vertically, and/or diagonally.) Good luck!

CAT • CAMEL • OX • DOLPHIN • SLED DOG • ELEPHANT • PIGEON • LLAMA • SHEEP • YAK • HORSE • DOG

A	L	E	E	P	L
M	O	N	T	E	Y
X	T	U	M	E	A
O	A	A	D	H	K
U	C	K	O	S	O
P	E	R	L	O	L
A	S	A	P	M	L
E	L	P	H	O	A
L	E	V	I	U	M
E	D	Q	N	F	A
P	D	A	B	A	D
H	O	R	O	P	B
A	G	O	D	O	P
N	O	E	G	I	P
T	A	L	E	T	A

Answers:

6 BORN TO BE WILD

All animals—even the ancestors of your favorite cat or dog—were wild animals once. Before any human beings came along, lots of animals roamed freely all over the Earth, adapting to their different environments. Some animals, such as the dinosaur, became extinct before we ever knew about them. People have different ideas about how this happened. Some scientists think that a big meteor hit the ground, producing a dark cloud that made the weather get too cold for these giant, cold-blooded reptiles. It's amazing to think that animals as big and strong as dinosaurs could disappear from the Earth completely. But they did.

"Oh, no, where did they all go?"

CAN YOU GUESS
. . . .

What has changed for the black rhino since the time you were born?

(Answer: In the past ten years—your lifetime, if you are ten years old or younger—27,000 rhinoceros have been killed. That leaves only 3,000 in all of Africa.)

How many wild animals can you find in this picture? How many of them live in your neighborhood?

DID YOU KNOW?

Scientists who study animal behavior are called "ethologists." Thanks to their work, we are learning about wild animal communities, including the life of elephants in the wild, their language and behavior. But, like so many other animals, elephants may be extinct before we really understand them.

Once there were millions of elephants roaming throughout Africa. Now, only 600,000 remain in all of Africa. That may seem like a lot, but if there's only one bad sickness, a terrible drought, or some other tragedy, those that still remain may not be able to survive.

If your mother had a baby, do you know how long she would be pregnant? Nine months. An elephant is pregnant

WILD NEIGHBORS
If you look carefully, you can see at least one wild animal in your backyard, near your school, or in your local park. Make a list of all the wild animals that live near you. What is in their environment— such as trash, other animals, cars, or pollution—that could make their lives dangerous?

for two years! And a female doesn't start having calves until it is fourteen or fifteen years old. So, even in the best of circumstances, it takes a long time for the elephant population to grow.

Rhinoceros, whales, wolves, birds of paradise, gorillas, and many other wonderful wild creatures could all become extinct by the year 2000. Once there were so many whales in the oceans of the world, sailors had to be careful not to bump into them. Now, after so much killing, many species are close to extinction. Wolves roamed all over North America and Europe. Now, they live in only a few places. The same is true of tigers, black-footed ferrets, and oryxes.

Throughout history species have become extinct naturally because their habitat or food source was destroyed. But, in the past two centuries humans have been speeding the destruction of one species after the next. And once these animals are gone, they will not be back. Extinction is forever.

ANIMALS IN TROUBLE

Men carrying automatic rifles plot the ambush. They will kill the old, the young, even mothers with babies. Their prize is great—"white gold" worth up to $240 a pound. The demand for white gold comes from all over the world. "Poachers" (people who hunt or steal animals illegally) are searching for this prize. It is their way of making a living. Is white gold a drug or a jewel? Not exactly—it is the beautiful white tusk of the elephant, which we call "ivory." Every day up to 200 elephants pay with their lives because of this human greed for ivory.

The poachers hack the tusks off the elephants' heads. Then the ivory is shipped out of Africa and carved into trinkets and jewelry. Instead of staying on the heads of magnificent wild elephants, the ivory may collect dust on someone's shelf.

You may have never seen a real, live elephant, but you

probably know that these wonderful animals live in Africa
or India. If the elephant becomes extinct, what will it be like
when your children ask you, "An elephant? What was that?"
That may sound strange to you now, but unless people
begin to act differently, your children may be asking you
that question about a lot of animals.

Over millions of years, many different animal species
have evolved with soft, warm fur, patterned skin, or bright,
colorful feathers. People like to wear these beautiful animal
furs and bird feathers, so they hunt and trap animals to get
them. And some people just like the sport of hunting.
People have often done whatever they pleased, no matter
how it hurts animals. But when people start to care, they
can make big changes.

Tuna fishing is an example of how caring people have
made a difference. Some tuna companies catch fish by
putting out huge nets in the sea. Dolphins get caught in
these nets and become injured or die. When the public
found out about this, many people refused to buy tuna. So

Poachers take wild animals from their natural homes.

some companies changed their way of fishing. Now you can buy "dolphin-safe" tuna, which is caught in ways that don't trap dolphins.

Hunting, trapping, and poaching are serious problems for the survival of wild animals. But humans cause other problems, too.

• **Destruction of habitat,** which you can read about in Chapter 2, is still a big one. The rainforests are disappearing so fast, it's scary to think about. But habitat is being destroyed closer to your home, too. Every time a shopping center, a housing development, or a dam is built, the environment is changed forever. Maybe you have seen the body of an animal that was killed on a highway. Lots of wild animals come down from the hills and out of forests in search of water or food the way they always have. But now there's a highway inbetween. Have you ever seen a sign that says deer crossing? It was a road for deer before it became a road for trucks.

• **Pollution** of the oceans, rivers, lakes, the air, and the beaches all affect wild animals. Oil spills do not just cover the surface of the water. They cover and kill some shore birds and sea mammals right away and then more slowly destroy the many smaller water animals. Have you ever been disappointed because the beach was closed for swimming because of pollution? You had the choice not to go in the water. Think about all the animals that don't have a choice.

• **Capturing wild animals** isn't as big a problem as it used to be, but wild animals are still sometimes captured for zoos, laboratories, and for the pet trade. Parrots, reptiles, and primates are all taken from their natural homes. For every infant chimpanzee that is captured alive, five others may be killed trying to protect the baby. Many animal babies also die on their way to captivity.

PROTECTOR PROFILE

JANE GOODALL (1934–   )

Imagine traveling to the other side of the world, to a deep, tropical jungle far away from your family and friends—all of this in the hope of seeing a chimpanzee. Then, once you were there, you would wake up every morning before dawn, crawl through the brush, climb up mountains, and sit quietly, waiting just to catch a glimpse of some chimpanzees. And what if you did that every day for weeks and months? That is exactly what Jane Goodall did.

When she began her research in 1960, women rarely

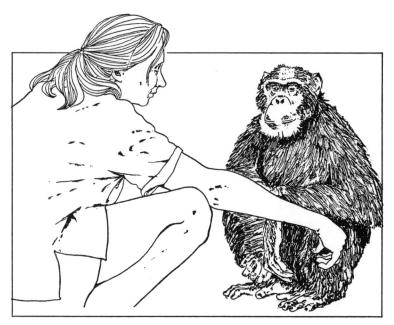

Jane Goodall made friends with chimpanzees in the wild.

went out alone to do field work like this. Nowadays there are many men and women ethologists who have studied animals in the wild. But Jane Goodall was the first person to make it her life's work to study a single species in the wild.

Jane Goodall grew up in England and was determined to go to Africa to see the animals there and learn everything she could about them. She worked to save up enough money for the trip to Africa. There, at the age of twenty-five, she met Louis Leakey, the famous anthropologist, and she worked with him for a year. Louis Leakey believed that there was much to be learned about early humans from studying the great apes in their natural habitat, and he thought Jane Goodall was the person to do it.

The young scientist traveled to the Gombe Stream Reserve in Tanzania. For the first eighteen months, she seldom saw chimpanzees close up. But she watched and waited, waited and watched, until the chimps got used to her and started to come out of the brush. With her patience and gentleness, Jane Goodall earned the trust of the chimpanzees, and she got to know them well.

Most wildlife studies go on for a year or two, only giving us a peek at an animal's life. But because Jane Goodall stayed and learned so much, we now know what happens when baby chimpanzees grow up, and about their life and death over generations. Through careful observation over thirty years, Jane Goodall and her students and helpers have learned that chimpanzees make and use tools and eat meat, that infants can die of grief if their mothers die, that there is war in the world of chimpanzees, and above all else, that family is important to these primates.

Chimps are now endangered. As an authority on chimpanzees, Jane Goodall has shared what she knows with people all over the world in order to protect the animals she has come to understand so well. When we come to know animals, we care about them. And Jane Goodall has made us care about what happens to chimpanzees.

 ## WHAT YOU CAN DO

❑ Speak up for animals. Let your friends and family know that you think buying a product made from an endangered species is contributing to animal extinction.

❑ Use recycled paper. Pulp and paper mills use chemicals that pollute the water where fish swim and other wild animals drink.

❑ Only buy dolphin-safe tuna, and tell your friends and family to read the labels on tuna cans.

❑ Contact groups that are working to save the rainforest and see what you can do to help.

WILD WORDS

- **Anthropologist**
- **Endangered**
- **Ethologist**
- **Ivory**
- **Poacher**

ACTIVITY:
FEATHERED-FRIEND FEEDERS

One way to make sure that you get to see wild birds up close is to place a bird feeder where you can see it through a window in your house. The birds will learn that they can find food at the feeder. They will visit it regularly and you can watch them eat. But once you start feeding them, you will need to continue. They will be counting on it.

When you decide where to place the feeder, make sure it is away from places where cats can hide and sneak up on the birds. If you don't want squirrels to share the birds' meals, protect the seeds by putting an aluminum pie plate on top of the feeder, or keep the squirrels away from the birds' food by giving them their own. Squirrels like cracked corn or bread.

FOR THE BIRDS. Wild birds eat many different foods. Seed-eaters, such as sparrows, will eat the birdseed sold at supermarkets and pet stores. You can also offer them peanut butter, especially in the winter when they need more fat in their diets. You can mix it with cornmeal or birdseed.

BIRD RESTAURANTS. There are many ways you can place food for the birds. Try making one of the easy feeders shown here. You may want to ask an adult to help you.

WINDOW TRAY
With this feeder, birds may come right up to your window. You will need:

• A flat board (about 1/2" thick and 18" square)
• Two feet of 1" x 1" stripping cut in two equal parts

- Edging (balsa wood will do)
- A hammer and nails

1. Put an edging around the flat board so the seeds won't blow off.
2. Nail in the supports at an angle.
3. Mount the tray outside on your window sill or just below.

If you're lucky, you can watch the birds with only the glass between you and them.

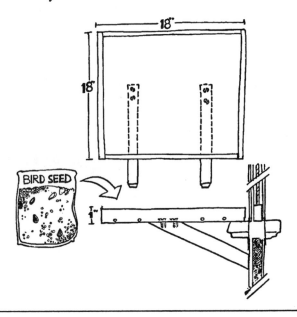

EASY FEEDER

For a really simple and natural birdfeeder, you can just use a big pinecone. First, attach a wire to the stem for a hanger. Then smear peanut butter between the pinecone scales and hang it up!

PEANUT BUTTER FEEDER

You will need:

- A small log, about 3" thick, or a 2" x 2" piece of wood, 12" long
- A screw eye
- A drill, or bottle caps and nails
- A wire for hanging
- A hammer

1. Drill 1" holes all along the wood. They can be pretty deep, but not all the way through.
2. Put a screw eye on one end of the log, so you can hang the feeder.
3. Fill the holes with a mixture of cornmeal and peanut butter.
4. Hang the feeder from a tree and watch as small birds and maybe even woodpeckers come to enjoy the treat.

If you don't have a drill, hammer bottle caps to the log. Fill the caps with peanut butter.

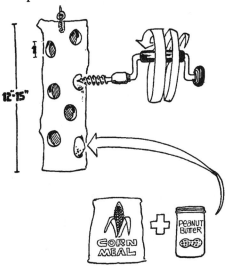

7 WHAT'S DOING AT THE ZOO?

Remember the last time you went to the zoo? Maybe you watched the monkeys swinging from the trees in an island exhibit or saw the elephants tossing hay around with their trunks. You might have seen the big teeth of a yawning hippopotamus or a giraffe nibbling leaves from a high branch. Most zoos do a wonderful job of caring for the animals that live there. They also work to keep endangered animals from becoming extinct.

But other zoos do not take such good care of the animals. Maybe you have seen a bear pacing back and forth in a small pen or a monkey just sitting and staring into space. That's how wild animals sometimes act when they are caged.

The best place for all wild animals to be is in their natural homes, and a zoo can never be that. But a zoo can protect animals when their natural habitat is threatened and when hunting and trapping are driving them to extinction.

? CAN YOU GUESS

. . . .

What makes a flamingo's feathers pink?

(Answer: In the wild, they eat shrimp. In the zoo, they eat carrots and shrimp shells. Shrimp, carrots, and other yellow vegetables contain carotene, which gives the birds their beautiful color.)

DID YOU KNOW?

"Zoo" is a short way of saying "zoological park." The first zoo in America was built in Philadelphia in 1872, and it's still there. Zoos are places where live animals are kept in captivity so people can see them on exhibit and learn more about them. Most zoos also want to conserve rare species. For most people, a trip to the zoo is the only way they will ever get close to a wild animal.

Good zoos feel responsible for the future of the animals in their care as well as in the wild. Zoo directors, curators, and veterinarians want to keep the wild animals healthy. They want the animals to reproduce to help them from becoming extinct. These experts often travel to an animal's native habitat to find out as much as they can about how to

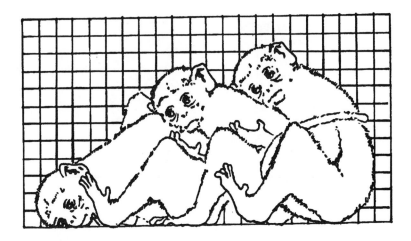

take care of the animals in the zoo and to help save the wild ones, too. Of course, the best ways to protect animals from extinction are to stop hunting and trapping them and to keep their natural habitats from being destroyed.

The best zoos have taken away the empty, boring cages they may have had in the past and replaced them with more natural, "humane" habitats. These exhibits include a variety of animal and plant species that are found together in the animal's natural home. An exhibit that looks more natural is a more interesting place for the animal to live and also helps teach visitors something about the natural habitat and behavior of the animal.

In the zoo, you can see what an animal looks like, but often you can't tell how it would behave if it were free—in its natural home. In captivity, lions are fed by zookeepers. In the wild, they are hunters, searching out and stalking their prey. Other animals forage all day for food, wandering across meadows or through forests munching on the plants that grow there. In a zoo, their food might be put in one spot. And some animals migrate, flying for miles above hills and trees. In the zoo, they might stay in the same place all year round. This is likely to change the way these wild animals behave. The normal territory of a wolf—if its habitat is not destroyed—might be as large as 200 square miles. When the wolf is confined to a small exhibit, its behavior is changed.

Don't fence me in

Have you ever wondered why chimpanzees don't escape from an island exhibit in a zoo? It's because they can't swim. A moat filled with water around an exhibit of great apes— such as gibbons, orangutans, chimpanzees, or gorillas—will keep them from leaving.

A pacing bear is a bored, unhappy bear.

ANIMALS IN TROUBLE

While the best zoos take good care of their animals, some zoos give animals very few of the things they need to be healthy and happy. Worst of all are the little roadside "zoos" and animal menageries that are set up just for money and make no effort to educate people or to protect animals in the wild. The owners of these places often don't care about the animals they put on display. They may keep the animals in prison-like conditions designed for the convenience of the people who take care of them and the people who come to see them.

Some bad zoos sell animals to laboratories for experiments. Some zoo animals even end up in "wild game" parks or hunting preserves where people pay thousands of dollars to shoot a lion or tiger at close range. Fortunately, most zoos are much better than that.

What's wrong with this picture?

PROTECTOR PROFILE: BRONX ZOO

BISON CONSERVATION PROGRAM

The story of saving the American bison is a success story for one wild animal and for the zoo that helped it survive. Without the efforts of The New York Zoological Society, this wonderful American bison would have been lost forever.

Once 60 million American bison roamed the prairies of the West. People who hunted bison for their hides and for sport, as well as for meat, reduced the herd to only a handful by 1907. The first director of the Bronx Zoo, William Hornaday, had 19 of the remaining bison brought to his zoo in New York. They lived there for several years

The Bronx Zoo helped save the American bison from extinction.

and began to have babies. Then 15 of the animals were sent to Oklahoma to start another herd. This was repeated several times. Today there are about 30,000 American bison living in protected areas in the United States, most descendants of the Bronx Zoo bison.

One sign of a good zoo is that it works cooperatively with other zoos to make certain that endangered animals are protected. When possible, a zoo will return animals to the wild, but it will not remove them from the wild. Now zoos have an international computer system. People in charge of certain species make sure that they know every animal of that species in captivity. This is the "species survival plan."

Planning for the survival of species is one of the good things that zoos do to protect animals. They are trying hard to be humane. Because many people got upset by the way animals were once treated in zoos, the American Association of Zoological Parks and Aquariums (AAZPA) was formed to set standards for zoos. All the best zoos are members.

By working cooperatively and by understanding endangered animals, zoos have been able to bring some of these animals back into the wild. The American bison, the red wolf, the Pere David deer, the oryx, the Przewalski horse, and the hog-nosed snake are a few species that might have become extinct if a few good zoos hadn't given them a second chance.

WHAT YOU CAN DO

❑ When you visit a zoo, read the signs. "Don't Feed the Animals" means what it says. Many animals are on special diets. Even though throwing them your potato chips or other "people food" might seem like fun, it could make the animal sick. Some zoos sell special food for feeding some animals, such as sea lions. But if you feed the animals this special food, don't tease them with it.

❑ Don't tease, try to scare, or shout at an animal in a zoo. Instead, see how much you can learn just by watching one animal. Is it watching you, too?

❑ Ask questions. One of the jobs of a zookeeper is to help you learn about animals.

❑ If you're on vacation and you see a zoo, check to see if it's a member of the American Association of Zoological Parks and Aquariums. Zoos that are members will post this information at the entrance.

❑ Visit a nature center or wildlife refuge to see wild animals in their natural habitat.

ACTIVITY:
ZOO EXHIBIT DIORAMA

Be a zookeeper—design a habitat. Choose a wild animal and read about it. What does it need to be healthy? Does it need to climb or swim? Is it diurnal or nocturnal? Research your animal thoroughly before you design your exhibit. If you can, visit your local zoo, museum, or aquarium to see how the animal you chose is exhibited. Can you think of a better exhibit design?

Here are some other questions you'll need to answer before designing your diorama:

- What is the theme of your exhibit? Are you highlighting a particular animal, habitat, or behavior?

- Is it an exhibit for one species of animal? Is it a mammal, bird, reptile, amphibian, or invertebrate?

- How much is known about your animal in its natural habitat? How and what does it eat? How would you feed your animals in a zoo exhibit?

- If you plan to exhibit several animals, how would you prevent the animals from hurting one another? Is there an area where the animals can go so visitors cannot see them, a place they can have some privacy? Is there a place where the animals can give birth and care for their young?

- If you choose to make your exhibit look like the animal's natural habitat, what materials will you use?

- What type of barrier will you use to separate the exhibit animals from the visitors (moat, glass, bars, wiring)?

- Is there any method you can use to make the animal more visible to the visitor without disturbing the animal's natural lifestyle?

- Most zoos use several different types of display arrangements including habitat (desert, grassland), geographic (North American, African), behavioral (nocturnal, burrowing), popular (great apes, elephants, giraffes), and themes for the many exhibits in the zoo.

How would you design a habitat?

How will your zoo be arranged?

After you've done your research, then you can design and construct your diorama. Here's what you'll need:

- Large shoe box
- Construction paper
- Cardboard
- Glue or paste
- Crayons and/or markers

- Pencils and paper
- Old magazines with pictures of animals
- Other materials as needed (rocks, twigs, leaves, etc.)

First, draw a landscape of your animal's environment on the inside of the box. Use your imagination to make the environment as natural-looking as you can. Then find pictures of the animals, glue them to the cardboard, and cut them out. Leave a piece of cardboard about 1" long on the bottom of the cut-out. Fold this piece back so the animal can stand up.

Make a label for your exhibit with the name of the animal, where it lives, what it eats, and any other information you have found out about it. Paste the label to the bottom front of the box. If everyone in your class or group makes a diorama, together you could make a whole zoo. Then invite your friends over to visit!

WILD WORDS

- Captivity
- Forage
- Humane
- Moat
- Territory
- Zoological park

8 THAT'S ENTERTAINMENT?

There is nothing like a good western movie. The cowboy and his horse gallop across the plains, over the rocky hillside, racing to get to the ranch before sundown. Suddenly the horse trips! Horse and rider fall. We know the cowboy is acting. But what about the horse?

You are at the circus. The huge tiger snarls and roars, and your palms get sweaty. The trainer in the middle of the ring cracks the whip commanding the cat to jump. But, he won't. He sits on his little stool, defiantly. The whip cracks again and the tiger swats at the seemingly defenseless human. Maybe this time he won't jump. But, once more the trainer commands. You hold your breath...the tiger leaps through a circle of fire.

Why would people want to watch a tiger jump through fire, or see horses fall? People call it entertainment. But it may not be fun for the animal.

CAN YOU GUESS

What canine went from starvation to sensation?

(Answer: The original Rin Tin Tin was a stray found by a soldier on a battlefield in France. He earned $6 million as an actor.)

DID YOU KNOW?

If you know the names Tom Cruise, the New Kids on the Block, and M. C. Hammer, then you probably know Lassie, Benji, Mr. Ed, and Flipper, too. They are all performers and celebrities. Animals are a big part of the entertainment industry. They perform on television shows, in commercials, on stage and in the movies. Horses, calves, and bulls are main attractions in a rodeo. And circuses almost always have animal acts—dogs, horses, elephants, and sometimes big cats.

It can be exciting to watch Lassie rescue a drowning boy on TV, and you may laugh to see a bear on roller skates or a chimpanzee smoking a big fat cigar in the circus. But the animal might not like it at all.

Horse races draw crowds all over the world. But each year during these races some horses fall and break their legs. There are also dog races. Well, someone might say, what's wrong with that? Greyhounds are bred to run, and they

ANIMAL ENTERTAINERS
Make a list of all the ways animals entertain people. And when you see an animal on TV, write down the name of the show or commercial.

"What do they think they're laughing at?"

probably like it. But, in fact, the dogs are trained to run by chasing live rabbits. If they don't run fast enough or win enough races they may be discarded by their owners.

Six heroes

Did you know that there were six generations of Lassie? The TV series, "Lassie," was based on six popular movies about the hero dog. And they all started with a book written in 1938.

ANIMALS IN TROUBLE

For some animals, being an entertainer can be very comfortable. Celebrity animals are often very well cared for and have trainers who love them. But then there are those that are misused and abused. Some animals, such as chimpanzees, are trained to act in different ways by being punished with electric shocks or beatings.

Although illegal in most of the United States, dog fights and cockfights are another form of "entertainment." These animals are trained to fight until they die. Other strange forms of animal entertainment include donkeys diving into pools from high platforms, dropping turkeys from airplanes,

and capturing rattlesnakes for sport.

Animals in the movies are another story. For a long time, there was no way to protect these animal actors. To make a fall look real, horses were tripped using wires stretched across their paths. They could not see the wire, and when they fell they were surprised and often badly hurt. Even though most people do their best to protect the animals on movie sets, some animals can still be hurt.

Did you ever see a rodeo? The horses buck because they have a strap fastened very tight on their bellies and they want to get it off because it is so uncomfortable. They are made to jump even higher with metal spurs. It is very frightening and painful for a calf to be roped and thrown to the ground.

Except for periods of time when they are being trained or performing, circus elephants are chained to a post. They travel all the time and are made to perform whether they feel like it or not. The more unnatural behaviors like balancing on a ball or standing on their heads cause injuries or diseases like arthritis.

PROTECTOR PROFILE

. . . .

RICHARD O'BARRY (1939–)

The former dolphin trainer for the "Flipper" television series and movie, Richard ("Ric") O'Barry now thinks that using dolphins as entertainers is wrong. Before working on the "Flipper" series, Ric O'Barry trained dolphins at the Miami Seaquarium. At first, he thought that capturing

dolphins and training them to perform for humans was a good way for people to learn about these friendly, intelligent animals. Over the years, however, he saw many dolphins suffer and die in captivity.

Ric O'Barry now works to teach people that dolphins don't belong in captivity. He encourages people who want to see dolphins to go where the dolphins live naturally and see them as they should be—free-swimming animals. He started a group called the Dolphin Project to help people as well as dolphins. The Dolphin Project helps people by teaching them about these wonderful aquatic mammals. And it helps trained dolphins by letting them "unlearn" their habits of human contact, so they can survive in the wild again.

In 1986, Ric O'Barry worked with Joe and Rosie, two dolphins that had been used in experiments on language. Joe and Rosie were no longer needed by the scientists. But because they had been in captivity for so long, they had forgotten how to catch fish for food and to swim fast in the ocean. Instead of just letting them be moved to another place of captivity, Ric O'Barry retrained them to take care of themselves. He taught them how to catch fish and survive in the wild again. And then he let them go, to live the rest of their lives as the free, wild animals they were born to be.

Ric O'Barry and the members of the Dolphin Project in Coconut Grove, Florida, are continuing their work. Their dream is to open some "dolphin halfway houses," where people can help more trained dolphins return to the wild again.

WHAT YOU CAN DO

❏ Do not go to any animal fights.

❏ If there are events in your town that abuse animals for entertainment, let people know that you think it is wrong.

❏ Look for a circus that doesn't use wild animals. Cirque du Soleil and The Pickle Family Circus are both a lot of fun with just human performers.

The Cirque du Soleil puts on a great show with only one kind of animal—humans.

CELEBRITY CHARADES

There have been many famous animals that have entertained us in movies, television, literature, and music. Many products, such as cars, and many sports teams are also named after animals. With several of your friends or classmates, see how many animal charades you can think of, act out, and guess in the following categories. Here are a few for starters. You can probably think of more.

BOOKS: *Charlotte's Web, Black Beauty*

CARTOONS: Pink Panther, Mickey Mouse

MOVIES: *The Bear, Lassie*

TELEVISION: Spuds McKenzie, Flipper

CARS: Mustang, Cougar

MUSICAL GROUPS: The Beatles, Stray Cats

SONGS AND NURSERY RHYMES: Old MacDonald's Farm
Hey Diddle Diddle

TEAMS NAMED FOR ANIMALS: Baltimore Orioles
Los Angeles Rams

PEOPLE DRESSED LIKE ANIMALS: Teenage Mutant Ninja Turtles
Big Bird

ACTIVITY: ORIGAMI

Animals have entertained people for centuries. For thousands of years, the Japanese have been entertaining their children by making animals out of paper. There are many wonderful origami books in your library or local bookstore with sample directions to follow.

Anyone can do origami because the only materials you need are some square pieces of paper. You can use old or recycled wrapping paper or plain bond paper, or you can buy origami paper at an art supply store.

To make an origami bird:

1. Take a square piece of origami paper. (The larger the square, the easier it is to work with it.) Fold your square into a triangle by folding it in half.

2. Unfold your triangle, hold it flat (working on the floor or a table) and turn your square around until it looks like a diamond.
   (Hint: the crease in the paper should be vertical—straight up and down).

3. Next, fold your diamond shape so that it looks like a kite or an ice cream cone. To do this take the point on each side and fold it over so each edge of the paper meets the crease in the center.

4. Follow the diagrams on the next page to complete your origami bird.

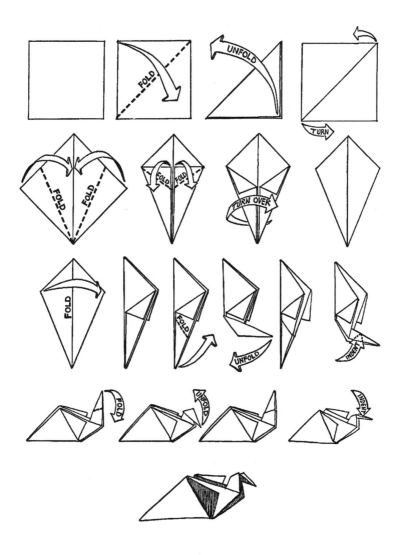

Follow these steps to make an origami bird.

9 BEAUTY AND THE MOUSE

nimals are used to test the safety of everything from face cream and cosmetics to furniture polish and paints. These tests are done to make sure that your skin or your eyes don't get irritated when you use these products.

 CAN YOU GUESS

Which products used to clean your house, your dishes, or yourself are tested on animals?

(Answer: All of them—unless they say on the label that they are not.)

DID YOU KNOW?

Companies don't have to use animals to find out if their products are safe for humans. Over the past few years, some cosmetics companies have switched to tests that don't use animals. Other companies use natural ingredients—such as oatmeal, aloe, lemon juice, cocoa butter, and other plant materials—that have been safely used by people for centuries and don't need to be tested at all.

In addition to being tested on animals, many cosmetics, such as lipstick and face cream, use ingredients like animal fat or turtle oil that come from animals. And hurting animals to make lipstick or moisturizer just isn't worth it.

"I wonder what's in this stuff anyway."

Using animals for medical research is another problem, and a harder one to solve. Everyone wants scientists to find cures for serious human diseases, such as AIDS, cancer, and heart disease. But people disagree about whether animals should be used in that research. Most people who care about protecting animals think that animals should be

used only if there is no other way to find out what the scientists need to know. And when scientists do use animals, they should use as few of them as possible, treat them as humanely as they can, and keep looking for new ways to do research that don't use animals.

Fortunately, many of the experiments that were once done on living animals can now be done using cells that can be grown in test tubes. Computers can even be used to find some of the answers. And many scientists are working to develop other new tests that don't use animals. Some people are also working to pass laws that will make companies stop testing on animals.

ANIMALS IN TROUBLE

Once, no one paid much attention to the way the rats, mice, monkeys, dogs, or even armadillos were used in the laboratory or the classroom. Millions and millions of crayfish, fetal pigs, cats, rats, frogs, and dogs were killed each year for use in school biology classes. Each year, about 5 million frogs are supplied for education or research. But as more people have started to speak out, greater effort has been made to find different ways to do these experiments, too.

Because many people prefer to buy products that are not tested on animals, some companies have started making "cruelty-free" cosmetics, lotions, soaps, and other products that are made without hurting animals. (Chapter 12 tells you how to order some of these cruelty-free beauty products.)

Thanks to computers, now you can study biology and save a frog, too.

PROTECTOR PROFILE
. . . .

SHEILA SCHWARTZ (1944–   )

Sheila Schwartz is the kind of teacher that we'd all like to have. She has a very funny sense of humor and enjoys teaching. And she loves to teach about animals and what kids can do to help them.

Because she wanted to help other teachers and students learn about the things they could do to help animals, Sheila Schwartz started the Humane Education Committee. Many teachers and other interested adults now belong to the Humane Education Committee and they share information on how to teach about animals.

The Humane Education Committee heard that students were required to dissect animals in biology classes, even though some of the students did not want to do so. Sheila contacted the Board of Education and, with the help of biologists and other teachers, was able to arrange alternative projects for students who would rather not dissect animals. Thanks to Sheila Schwartz and the Humane Education Committee, any student in the city of New York can choose to learn about biology using a computer program or model instead of dissecting a frog or other animal.

 ## WHAT YOU CAN DO

❏ If you'd like more information on alternatives to dissection, contact your local humane society or write to the ASPCA education department. (The address is in Chapter 12.)

❏ If you'd like to do a science project about animals, study the behavior of wild animals without disturbing them, or study the behavior of your pet. You can get more information on humane biology projects from the ASPCA education department.

❏ Try using a combination of baking soda and vinegar to clean sinks and counters. Vinegar and water will do a great job making your windows sparkle.

❏ You can make all sorts of beauty products from natural materials you have at home. If you get too much sun, try rubbing your skin with the inside of an aloe plant, cucumbers, or strawberries (as long as you're not allergic to them).

ACTIVITY: HOMEMADE HELPERS

Many of the products people use at home are tested on animals. Even after these products have been tested, many can still harm us or the environment because they contain toxic ingredients. Ask your parent or another adult to help you make some of your own household cleaners from natural, nontoxic ingredients instead.

Oven Cleaner:
• 2 cups baking soda
• 6 cups water
• Scouring pad

Disinfectant:
• Dissolve 1/2 cup borax in one gallon of hot water
• Sponge

Floor and Furniture Polish:
• 1 part lemon juice
• 2 parts vegetable oil
• Rag

MAKE YOURSELF BEAUTIFUL

Most shampoos contain preservatives derived from petrochemicals and formaldehyde. These can have harmful effects such as burning and irritating your eyes. Try making your own shampoo from natural ingredients.

Natural Shampoo:
• Aloe (from health-food store or pharmacy)
• Almond extract (grocery or health-food store)
• Coconut oil (grocery or health-food store)
• Citric acid or lemon juice (grocery store)

Mix all ingredients together. Change the amount of

water, aloe, and almond extract depending on the smell you like and how much shampoo you want to make. Rinse your hair with cool water. Now you are squeaky clean!

Oven Cleaner:

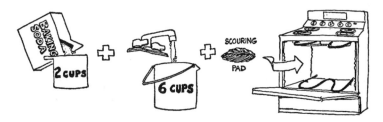

Floor and Furniture Polish:

Disinfectant:

WILD WORDS

• Cruelty-free   • Dissection

10 FASHIONABLE FURS ARE FAKE

F ur is wonderful to touch. If you have a cat, you know how nice it feels to stroke your pet's fur. And if you've ever cuddled against someone wearing a fur coat, you know how soft and warm that can be, too. But did you ever think about where the beautiful, soft fur came from before it was made into a person's coat? Maybe it came from animals raised on ranches for their fur. And maybe it came 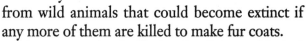 from wild animals that could become extinct if any more of them are killed to make fur coats.

Some people think that having a rabbit's foot is good luck. It's certainly not good luck for the rabbit!

 CAN YOU GUESS

· · · · · · · · · · · · · · · · · · · ·

How many minks does it take to make one small mink coat?

(Answer: 65!)

DID YOU KNOW?

. . . .

No one in our society today needs fur to keep warm. We have many other kinds of materials to choose from when we buy coats, jackets, and blankets. We can even buy the patterns of wild animals with fashionable fake fur.

Many centuries ago in places where the winters were cold—and even now in some parts of the world—animals such as bears and wolves were trapped for the warmth of their fur. The beautiful patterns and textures of furs soon made them very valuable and many people wanted to have them for their beauty as well as their warmth. Owning a fur coat soon became a status symbol, and the demand was very great for this expensive kind of clothing.

Trapping wild animals is hard work. It takes a lot of time, too, since many "pelts" are needed to make just one coat. So the business of fur ranching was started to raise animals for their fur. Today, more than half of the animals used for fur coats are raised on ranches. Rabbits, foxes, chinchillas, and minks are the animals most often raised in this way.

CHECK OUT YOUR CLOSET

Look at the clothes in your closet—your sweaters, coats, and jackets. Read the labels. Make a list of the clothes made from animals. What other materials could have been used instead?

ANIMALS IN TROUBLE

Some exotic animals—like the jaguar, ocelot, leopard, and lynx—are still being trapped to make fur coats and jackets. The animals are caught using a leg-hold trap, which closes around the animal's leg. To top it off, other animals, such as rare birds, are captured for their feathers to decorate hats and fancy dresses. And alligators and other reptiles are killed to make purses and shoes.

Trappers say they help control the population of some animals. But, in fact, trapping has almost driven the lynx and wolf to extinction. Trappers say they keep the population under control because they kill animals that are weak or sick. But, in fact, weak animals don't move around a lot, so it is the healthy ones that are usually caught in the traps.

Trapping wild animals for their fur is just plain cruel.

As many as 17 million animals were trapped in 1986, and 4 million in 1990. The number of animals trapped is becoming fewer and fewer because people are buying less fur now that they know how many rare and wonderful species are being threatened by it.

 PROTECTOR PROFILE

BEAVER DEFENDERS: HOPE AND CAVIT BUYUKMIHCI

Hope and Cavit Buyukmihci were a young couple who wanted to live a simple life close to nature where they could raise their children surrounded by trees and wildlife. They searched and searched for the right place. Finally, in 1961, they found 85 acres of wooded swampland in rural New Jersey. It had a shack that would become their home and a pond that was already home to a family of beavers. They named their new home Unexpected Wildlife Refuge.

Over the years, Hope became very fond of the beavers that lived on the land. She watched them working to build their dams out of wood and mud. Hope found them to be intelligent, gentle, and industrious. And she was shocked to discover that even on their "refuge," these wild animals, among others, were not safe. Trappers were trying to capture them for their fur.

Hope and her husband put up signs on their Unexpected Wildlife Refuge prohibiting hunting and trapping, but the hunters and trappers didn't stop. The Buyukmihcis could not stand by and watch their animal friends hurt. So they began to walk the land, blowing whistles to scare away the animals so hunters would not be able to find them. They took trespassers to court. But even then, the hunters and trappers were usually not punished. So, the Unexpected Wildlife Refuge fought back by buying more land to protect the beavers. The refuge is now 400 acres.

In 1970, Hope and many other people who are concerned about the beavers' survival formed a group called Beaver Defenders. They work to protect these animals and educate people about the need to care for all wildlife. Now, at least the beavers living in the Unexpected Wildlife Refuge have a better chance of living a natural life without the threat of a steel-jaw leg-hold trap ending their lives.

WHAT YOU CAN DO

❑ When you want to stay warm, look for something to wear that's not made with fur.

❑ If you wear fake fur, make sure people know it is not real. Wear a "fake fur" button on your coat.

I WEAR FAKE FUR

❑ Let people know what you have learned about how animals suffer when they are trapped and when they are raised on farms and ranches for their fur.

ACTIVITY: FAKE-FUR MAGNETS

To make fake-fur refrigerator magnets you will need:

- Magazine pictures of animals with fur
- Cardboard
- Pencil
- Scissors
- Cotton balls, fake-fur scraps, or yarn
- Buttons for eyes
- Glue
- A small magnet for each animal

1. Cut out a picture of a furry animal from a magazine.
2. Trace around the picture onto a piece of cardboard. (Or draw your own animal.)
3. Cut out the cardboard animal and the fake fur to match.
4. Glue the fake fur, cotton balls, yarn, and buttons to the cut-out. Use your imagination!
5. Glue a small magnet to the back of the cardboard. Let it dry.
6. Stick your fake-fur magnet to your refrigerator.

WILD WORDS

- **Leg-hold trap**
- **Refuge**
- **Pelt**
- **Trapper**

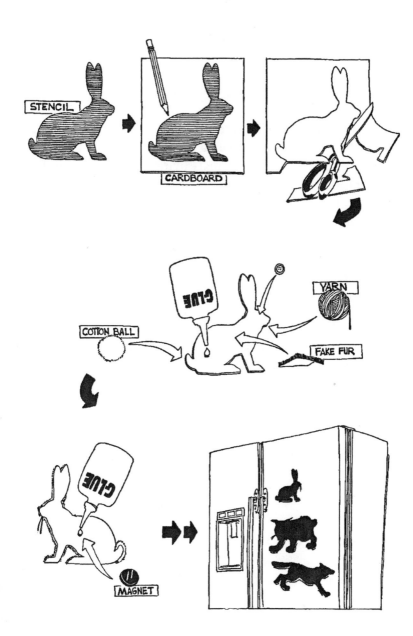

11 DOWN ON THE FARM

U nless you live on or near a farm, you may never have seen a real farm animal. There are many different kinds of animals living on farms, including pigs, chickens, cows, and sheep. These animals, called "livestock," are raised to provide people with food and materials to make clothing, among other things. Whether or not you and your family use some of the products raised from animals on farms, you will be surprised to learn some interesting facts about them, and about some of the problems they face.

CAN YOU GUESS
. . . .

What do Rhode Island Reds, Bantams, and Leghorns have in common?

(Answer: They are all chickens.)

DID YOU KNOW?

All chickens are descended from the "red jungle fowl" of the Far East. Like the jungle fowl, domestic chickens will live in small groups when given the chance. The males (called "cocks") protect the females (called "hens") and their chicks. Chickens look for food by scratching in the dirt for seeds, grain, and insects. They also enjoy ruffling their feathers and covering themselves with very fine soil or dust. This is called "dust bathing" and helps keep insects off their skin.

Cattle (cows and bulls) were probably domesticated as long as 7,000 years ago. They played an important role in

FARM FAMILIES
Match the name of the male, female, and offspring of different farm animals.

MALE	FEMALE	OFFSPRING
1. a. Ram	a. Hen	a. Calf
2. b. Cock	b. Ewe	b. Piglet
3. c. Boar	c. Cow	c. Chick
4. d. Bull	d. Sow	d. Lamb

(Answers: 1. a-b-d; 2. b-a-c; 3. c-d-b; 4. d-c-a)

the development of civilization as humans changed from a society of hunters and gatherers to a society that depended on agriculture. People began raising cattle for meat so they didn't have to hunt for it. They used the cow's milk to make butter, cheese, and yogurt. The horns, bones, and skins were used to make tools and clothing. Some cattle were even used to help pull the plows used to prepare fields for planting. In some cultures, wealth is measured by how many cattle a person owns. In other cultures, cows are "sacred." They are allowed to walk around the streets, and no one owns them or eats them.

Pigs are probably the most intelligent animals found on a farm. They can learn many of the same things that a dog can learn. Even though we may say that someone eats like a pig, or is as dirty as a pig, pigs will not overeat when left on their own, and are really quite clean. When pigs do wallow or roll in mud during the summer, they do it to keep cool.

ANIMALS IN TROUBLE

Just like the many other animals you have read about in this book, the animals on farms face problems as well. Even though we may see or think about chickens walking around and scratching for food, cows contentedly munching grass in a pasture, or pigs cooling themselves in the mud, this is not the case for many farm animals.

Today, fewer and fewer people work on farms, but more animals are being raised for food. So lots of animals are kept in confined, crowded conditions with fewer people to take

care of them. Chickens that live in cages are prevented from scratching, dust bathing, or even stretching their wings. Pigs seldom have a chance to shuffle and grunt in a field or use a mud hole to cool off. Instead, they are raised in barns with concrete floors. Some calves that are raised to become veal may be taken from their mothers when they are just one or two days old and put in pens so small that they are not even able to turn around.

Because the animals raised under these crowded conditions may be treated more like machines than animals, places that use these methods are sometimes called "factory farms." Factory farms prevent the animals raised there from being able to do many of the things they would do naturally.

PROTECTOR PROFILE

ASTRID LINGREN (1907–)

Pippi Longstocking is a character you may know. Several books have been written about this smart and mischievous girl. She is a character who thinks for herself and often surprises us. Pippi makes us laugh and makes us think—just like the writer who created her, Astrid Lingren.

Astrid Lingren spent a happy childhood, in a community of small family farms in Sweden. The cows, horses, sheep, and pigs were all her friends. Her family loved their animals and cared well for them until the time when they had to be killed for food. When she grew up,

Writer Astrid Lingren helped improve life for farm animals in Sweden.

Astrid Lingren moved to the city of Stockholm, took a job in a publishing company, and also began her writing career. She wrote many books and stories for and about children. Many of her stories take place in the countryside where she was so happy.

In the 1960s, Sweden began to replace small family farms with factory farms. Astrid Lingren was shocked to hear her beloved pigs, cows, and chickens called "production units." She was sad about the way they had to live their short lives and how producing more animals for meat was changing life for people as well. She wrote an article about the cows she loved for a big Swedish newspaper. The article told about the way cows had to live on factory farms.

She continued to write articles and stories about the way farm animals were being treated. Other people began speaking up, too. Soon, the people of Sweden began pressuring their government to pass laws protecting the rights of the animals. In 1988, legislation was passed giving cows grazing rights, forbidding pigs to be tied up, and assuring that they must have separate places for bedding and for eating. Chickens had to be let out of their cramped cages, and no animals living on the farm could be given drugs or hormones except to treat disease. Even when the animals go to slaughter, the law says it must be done as "humanely as possible."

Hopefully, the rest of the European countries and the United States will follow Sweden's example. Astrid Lingren believes that "animals have the right for a decent life during the short time they have on this earth. Animals can feel pain and sorrow and agony, and the fear of death, just as we do. Every human being who has a heart knows that, really." Astrid Lingren made people think. And when people think, they can act.

WHAT YOU CAN DO

❑ If you and your family are shopping for meat, try to find organic and "free-range" meats. Look for these meats at health-food stores, farmers' markets, or even at some big grocery stores.

❑ Try adding more grains, vegetables, and legumes—such as wheat corn, rice, nuts, peas, and beans—to your diet. Eating more fiber to lower your cholesterol is good for your health, and it reduces the need to raise so many farm animals in crowded conditions.

WILD WORDS

• Livestock   • Factory farm   • Free-range

ACTIVITY: SPROUTING SPROUTS

Sprouts are a wonderful food. They are seeds that have just begun to grow. Sprouts have a lot fiber, lots of nutrition and they are very low in calories. Alfalfa and mung beans are the most popular kinds of seeds to sprout at home. They are also very easy to grow. You can harvest a fresh crop of bean sprouts in less than a week. Try them in sandwiches, in omelettes, in stir fry, and in salads. You can buy a "sprouting jar" all set to go at a health-food store, but it is easy and fun to make your own.

ALFALFA SPROUTS

What you will need:
- 4 tablespoons alfalfa seeds
- A mason jar
- Cheesecloth
- Rubber band
- Water

1. Measure the seeds and put them into the jar.
2. Cover the jar with the cheesecloth.
3. Fill the jar halfway with water.
4. Soak the seeds for 4-6 hours (overnight is good).
5. Drain all the water. Make sure it is all out.
6. Rinse the sprouts 2 times a day. Each time, make sure the water is drained out completely. Keep the jar near a window for some light.
7. Watch the seeds sprout. When they are a nice light green, eat them! They will keep in the refrigerator for several days.
8. Start a new batch.

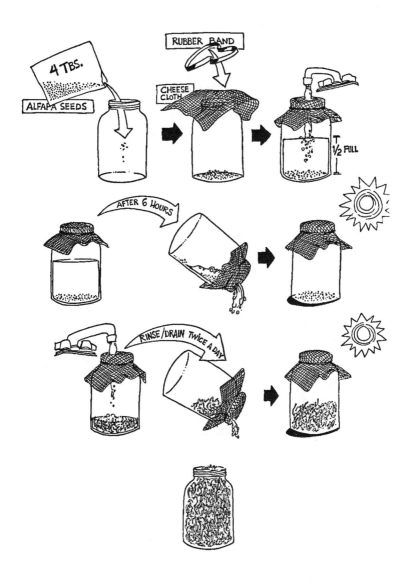

Follow the directions on these pages to grow your own sprouts.

MUNG SPROUTS

Mung sprouts are a bit different and need to stay in the dark. Otherwise, follow the steps above. Mung sprouts will be 1-1/2" long when they are ready and are sweet to eat.

GROWING A RADISH GARDEN

You will need:
- Empty milk carton
- Scissors
- Plastic wrap
- Masking tape
- Soil
- Radish seeds (a garden shop will carry them)

1. Cut out a 3" strip from one side of the milk carton from the bottom to halfway up the side. (This will be your peephole.)
2. Cover this rectangular hole with plastic wrap and tape down the edges with masking tape.
3. Fill the carton with damp soil and put several radish seeds in the soil.
4. Place the carton near a sunny window.
5. Keep the soil damp, but not soggy.
6. In two or three days, the radishes should start to grow. If they get too crowded, pull some out to give the biggest ones room to grow.
7. When your radishes are big enough to pick, get ready for a tangy bite of home-grown radish.
8. Try eating them with your sprouts—maybe on a dolphin-safe tuna sandwich.

12 MORE TO LEARN: RESOURCES

Many organizations, large and small, are working in the United States and throughout the world to protect animals. Since we cannot list all of them, we have included a small selection that may provide educational materials about specific topics.

HUMANE ORGANIZATIONS

Alliance for Animals, P.O. Box 909, Boston, MA 02103

American Anti-Vivisection Society, 801 Old York Road, Suite 204, Jenkintown, PA 19046

American Humane Association, 9725 East Hampden Ave., Denver, CO 80231

"I never knew there was so much to learn about us animals!"

American Humane Education Society, 350 S. Huntington Ave., Boston, MA 02130

The American Society for the Prevention of Cruelty to Animals (ASPCA), 441 E. 92nd St., New York, NY 10128

Animal Welfare Institute, P.O. Box 3650, Washington, DC 20007

Friends of Animals, P.O. Box 1244, Norwalk, CT 06856

Humane Education Committee, P.O. Box 445, New York, NY 10019

Humane Society of the United States, 2100 L St., NW, Washington, DC 20015-0516

National Anti-Vivisection Society, 53 West Jackson Blvd., Chicago, IL 60604

WILDLIFE AND CONSERVATION GROUPS

Here are some of the groups that have information on wildlife and conservation. Ask them if they oppose sport hunting. If they don't, tell them how you feel about protecting wildlife.

American Association of Zoological Parks and Aquariums (AAZPA), Oglebay Park, Wheeling, WV 26003

The Beaver Defenders, Unexpected Wildlife Refuge, Newfield, NJ 08344

The Cousteau Society, Inc., 930 West 21st St., Norfolk, VA 23517. (804) 627-1144

Defenders of Wildlife, 1244 19th St., NW, Washington, DC 20036

The Jane Goodall Institute, P.O. Box 41720, Tucson, AZ 85717

National Audubon Society, 950 Third Ave., New York, NY 10020. (212) 832-3200

National Wildlife Federation, 1400 16th St., NW, Washington, DC 20036. (202)797-6800

Natural Resources Defense Council, 40 W. 20th St., New York, NY 10011. (212) 727-2700

The Nature Conservancy, 1815 N. Lynn St., Arlington, VA 22209. (703) 841-5300

Rainforest Action Network, 301 Broadway, Suite A, San Francisco, CA 94133. (415) 398-4404

Sierra Club, 730 Polk St., San Francisco, CA 94109. (415) 776-2211

Wildlife Conservation International, 185 St. and Southern Blvd., Bronx, NY (212) 220-5155

Wildlife Refuge Reform Coalition, P.O. Box 18414, Washington, DC 20036-8414. (202) 778-6145

World Wildlife Fund, 1250 24th St., NW, Washington, DC 20037. (202) 293-4800

GREAT BOOKS ABOUT ANIMALS

Animal Rights by Patricia Curtis, MacMillan, 1980
*The Animal Rights Handbook: Everyday Ways to Save Animals'
    Lives.* Living Planet Press, 1990
Black Beauty by Anna Sewell. Crown Publishers, 1988
Charlotte's Web by E. B. White. Buckineer Books, 1990
Crusade for Kindness: Henry Bergh and the ASPCA by John J.
    Loeper, Atheneum, 1991
Forgotten Animals by Linda Koebner. Dutton, 1984
The Incredible Journey by Sheila Burnford. Bantam, 1990
Julie of the Wolves by Jean Craighead George. Harper
    Collins, 1972
The Jungle Books by Rudyard Kipling. Viking, 1987
Lily Pond: Four Years with a Family of Beavers by Hope
    Ryden. William Morrow & Co., Inc., 1989
Much Ado About Aldo by Johanna Hurwitz. Puffin, 1989
My Life with the Chimpanzees by Jane Goodall. Minstrel,
    1988
The Ocean World by Jacques-Yves Cousteau. Harry N.
    Abrams, Inc., 1979
Watership Down by Richard Adams. Avon, 1977
Zoobooks, published quarterly by Wildlife Education Ltd.

MAGAZINES

Kind News and *Children and Animals*, National Association
    for the Advancement of Humane and Environmental
    Education, P. O. Box 362, East Haddam, CT 06423
Junior Report, ASPCA, 441 East 92 St., New York, NY
    10128
National Geographic World, The National Geographic
    Department, 17th and M Streets, NW, Washington, DC
    20036

VIDEOS

More and more videos are now being produced. Many of the organizations listed on pages 129 to 131 may have them. One wonderful resource for videos is Focus on Animals, P.O. Box 150, Trumbull, CT 06611. You may also write to the ASPCA and to the Cousteau Society to request information about their videos.

List of ASPCA Videos:

"Good Dogs, Great Owners." Brian Kilcommons shows you how to train your canine companion. ($29.95)

"The Other Side of the Fence." Discusses factory farming, using veal calves as an example. ($69.95)

"The Price They Pay." Considers the costs of trapping and wildlife exploitation in terms of animal suffering. ($69.95)

"A Question of Respect." Looks at the use of animals in research, testing, and education. ($69.95)

"Throwaways." Promotes spaying and neutering of cats and dogs to deal with the problem of pet overpopulation. ($15.00)

MORE INFORMATION ABOUT
SPECIFIC SUBJECTS

COMPANION ANIMALS

For information on low-cost spaying and neutering, call:
Spay-Neuter USA, 1-800-248-SPAY

For more information on companion animals, write:
Association of Veterinarians for Animal Rights, P.O.
  Box 6269, Vacaville, CA 95696

ALTERNATIVES TO DISSECTION

"Operation Frog" is a computer software program that
simulates the dissection and reconstruction of the frog using
proper sequence and instruments. It is available from
Scholastic Software, Inc., P.O. Box 7502, 2931 East
McCarty St., Jefferson City, MO 65102. For more
information, call 1–800–922–FROG.

CRUELTY-FREE BEAUTY AND CLEANING PRODUCTS

Write or call for an updated list of cruelty-free cosmetics:

Beauty without Cruelty USA, 175 W. 12th St., Suite 15G, New York, NY 10128-8275. (212) 989-8073

The Body Shop, Hanover Technical Center, 45 Horsehill Road, Cedar Knolls, NJ 07927-2003. (201) 984-9200

Ecco Bella, 125 Pompton Plains Crossroad, Wayne, NY 07470. (201) 890-7077

John Paul Mitchell Systems, P.O. Box 10597, Beverly Hills, CA 90213. (805) 298-0400

Shopper's Guide to Cruelty-Free Products, P.O. Box 22505, Sacramento, CA 95822

Tom's of Maine, Railroad Ave., Kennebunk, ME 04042

FARM ANIMALS

Farm Animal Reform Movement, 10101 Ashburton Lane, Bethesda, MD 20817

Farm Sanctuary, P.O. Box 150, Watkins Glen, NY 14891

Food Animal Concerns Trust, P.O. Box 14599, Chicago, IL 60614

Humane Farming Association, 1550 California St., Suite B, San Francisco, CA 94109

GLOSSARY

Anthropologist: A person who studies the different cultures, customs, and behaviors of human beings.

Breed: 1. To mate in order to produce babies. 2. A certain kind of animal within a species. (A beagle is a breed of dog.)

Canine: Of the dog family.

Captivity: Being kept somewhere, not free.

Carnivore: A meat-eating animal; a predator, such as a lion.

Cold-blooded: Having a body temperature that changes with the temperature of the environment outside. (Reptiles are cold-blooded.)

Companion animal: A pet, an animal friend.

Cruelty-free: Cosmetics or other household products made and tested without using animals.

Dissection: Cutting apart or dividing in order to study something.

Diurnal: Active during the day.

Domesticate: To tame or train an animal so it can live with or work with humans.

Ecosystem: A community of all the plants and animals in an area together with its physical environment, and how they work together as a whole.

Endangered: In danger of becoming extinct.

Environment: All the conditions in an area; surroundings.

Ethologist: A scientist who studies the natural behavior of animals.

Euthanize: The act of putting to death painlessly; to cause a "gentle death."

Evolution: The idea that groups of living things, such as species, change over time, making future generations different from the ones that came before.

Exoskeleton: A hard outside structure that protects or supports many invertebrates, such as insects.

Extinction: No longer existing; every one of a certain species or group being dead.

Factory farm: A place where large numbers of animals are raised for food in overcrowded conditions.

Food chain: The natural connection between plants and animals in which a plant-eating animal is eaten by a meat-eating animal, and so on.

Forage: To search for food.

Free-range: An animal raised for food that is not kept in a cage, but is free to move about, such as a free-range chicken.

Habitat: The region or area where an animal or plant species lives.

Herbivore: A plant-eating animal, such as a cow.

Homing pigeon: A domestic pigeon that will always return to its home roost, and can be used to carry messages great distances.

Humane: To be kind; merciful.

Invertebrate: An animal without a backbone, such as insects, jellyfish, and crabs.

Ivory: The hard, smooth, yellowish-white tusk of an elephant or walrus, taken from the animal by humans to make jewelry or other objects.

Leg-hold trap: A steel trap that closes down on an animal's leg, used to catch wild animals for their fur.

Livestock: Domestic animals, such as cows and sheep, raised to work or to make a profit for their owners.

Mammary gland: The milk-producing organ of female mammals.

Marsupial: A kind of mammal, including kangaroos and koalas, that keeps its young in a pouch on the front of the mother's body after the animal is born.

Migration: The movement of animals from one part of the world to another during certain seasons of the year.

Moat: A ditch surrounding an island and often filled with water, commonly used in zoo exhibits to keep the animals from leaving.

Monotreme: A mammal that lays eggs instead of giving birth to live babies.

Neuter: To remove the reproductive organs of a male animal to prevent it from breeding; to alter.

Nocturnal: Active at night.

Nomadic: Wandering from place to place; without a permanent home.

Oceanography: The exploration and study of oceans, including the plants and animals there.

Omnivore: An animal that can eat and digest both plants and animals. (Humans are omnivores.)

Overpopulation: Too many animals in an area; over-crowding so that the food and space of an area is used up.

Pelt: The skin of an animal with the fur still on it.

Pesticide: A chemical used to kill pests, especially bugs on human food.

Pet: An animal kept by humans for companionship.

Poacher: A person who hunts or fishes illegally.

Pollinate: To transfer pollen from the male to the female part of a plant or flower, allowing the plant to form seeds.

Predator: An animal that hunts and kills other animals for food. (Owls are predators of mice.)

Prey: An animal that is hunted or caught by other animals for food. (Mice are prey for owls.)

Puppy mill: A place where dogs are kept in overcrowded conditions and bred to produce large numbers of puppies.

Rainforest: A dense forest that receives at least 100 inches of rain each year and is home to many special plants and animals.

Refuge: A protected place. (An animal refuge provides animals with a safe home.)

Rodeo: A competition for entertainment in which people ride horses and bulls and rope calves.

Seeing Eye dog: A dog trained to lead a blind person.

Spay: To remove the ovaries of a female animal to prevent pregnancy; to alter.

Species: A specific type of animal or plant which can reproduce with other members of the same type. (An eagle is a species of bird.)

Symbiosis: The close relationship of two or more different animals, which is usually helpful to each.

Territory: An area inhabited by an animal or group of animals, which they will often fight to defend.

Thorax: The second or middle region of an insect's body; the part of a human body between the neck and ribcage.

Trapper: A person who catches animals for their fur.

Vertebrate: An animal with a backbone.

Veterinarian: A doctor who treats animals.

Warm-blooded: Having a warm body temperature that stays the same, even when the temperature of the outside environment changes. (Mammals are warm-blooded.)

Zoological park (zoo): A place where living animals are kept and exhibited to the public.

Zoologist: A scientist who studies animals.

ABOUT THE AUTHOR

Linda Koebner grew up in a house full of animals, and animals have always been an important part of her life. She has had the opportunity to observe animals in the wild and also to share her enthusiasm for them with others. She has worked in the departments of animal behavior at the American Museum of Natural History and at Cambridge University in England. She has also worked with the New York Zoological Society and Wildlife Conservation International. Linda has written two other books about animals, *From Cage to Freedom* and *Forgotten Animals*. The author now lives in Riverdale, New York, with her son, Ian, her best friend, Ron, six cats, and two dogs.

ABOUT THE ILLUSTRATOR

Cartoonist/illustrator **Thomas C. Whittemore** studied animal behavior at Harvard University. While in search of vervet monkeys, Thomas met Linda Koebner on an island full of sugar plantations, mangoes, and voodoo. They have been friends ever since. Thomas has been a railroad gandy dancer, an oil doodlebugger, a tramp-freighter deckhand, and an ape observer. He received a master's degree in physical anthropology at the University of Chicago. He now lives in Seattle. His cartoons and illustrations regularly appear in Northwest publications and across the nation.

ABOUT THE EDITORS

Michael E. Kaufmann is Director of Education for the ASPCA. He has been fascinated by animals since his father took him to the zoo when he was a child. Now his job is to teach other people about animals, about nature, and about how people can take care of all living things.

Stephen Zawistowski, Ph.D., holds a doctorate in psychology and genetics and is Vice President for Humane Education for the ASPCA. He grew up in a small town on Lake Erie and got to know the many animals living nearby. One of the first words he learned to spell was "zoologist," which is what he grew up to be.

ABOUT THE ASPCA

The American Society for the Prevention of Cruelty to Animals (ASPCA), America's first humane society, was founded in 1866 to provide effective means for the prevention of cruelty to animals throughout the United States. Today, with over 400,000 members nationwide, the ASPCA helps animals through education, legislation, and law enforcement programs. In addition, through shelter, adoption, animal rescue, and veterinary programs in New York City, the ASPCA provides hands-on care to more than 125,000 animals each year.

PLEASE JOIN US!

If you like this book, you will probably like the **ASPCA Junior Report**, too. It's a newsletter just for kids who love animals, and it's full of lots of activities and information about animals everywhere. Just ask your parent to fill out the form below and send it to us, and we'll send you a free 3-month-trial family membership in the ASPCA, which includes the **Junior Report.**

QTY	ITEM	UNIT PRICE	TOTAL
	3-month trial membership	**Free**	
	Special offer **1-year family membership**	**$25.00** **(regularly $30.00)**	
	Additional copies of ***FOR KIDS WHO LOVE ANIMALS***	**$6.95**	
* Please include $1.50 for each copy of *FOR KIDS WHO LOVE ANIMALS*		**POSTAGE***	
		TOTAL	

Please make your check or money order payable to: **ASPCA**
     ASPCA
     Family Membership Offer
     CN 2041
     Toms River, NJ 08754-2941

❏ I am not able to join, but would like to make a contribution of $_____

❏ Please send me more information about ASPCA programs.

PARENT'S NAME _____

ADDRESS_____

CITY _____ STATE _____ ZIP _____

CHILD'S NAME_____

CHILD'S BIRTHDATE _____
                             month / day / year